Working in Real Organizations

Working in Real Organizations

Michael Watts and Matthew Glew

Collins Educational

An Imprint of HarperCollins*Publishers*

Published in 1994 by Collins Educational
An imprint of HarperCollins*Publishers*
77–85 Fulham Palace Road
Hammersmith
London
W6 8JB

British Library Cataloguing in Publication Data is available from the British Library.

ISBN 0–00–322359–0

Cover illustration by Chris Price
Printed in Great Britain by

Contents

Introduction

Aim

Working in Real Organizations exactly meets the needs of business students following A/AS level courses, the BTEC National Awards and the Advanced GNVQ in Business. It is designed to help students relate business studies to real-world situations, stimulating their interest in the subject and encouraging them to look beyond the immediate confines of the syllabus. The book is presented in a way that encourages students to apply business concepts and ideas to the real business world.

Content

The book covers the most essential elements that lie within the syllabuses to a level that allows the book to be used as complementary to other texts. As a classroom resource the book will help to take the pressure of research and preparation off the teacher or lecturer; it contains the all-important material needed to shift the focus from the syllabus to the real world of business.

Each of the book's eight units is based upon an industrial or commercial organization that will be familiar to students. We selected the organizations because they are particularly appropriate vehicles for the development and analysis of the respective parts of the syllabus. The selection also acknowledges the interests and awareness of young people as potential consumers and/or part-time employees. In addition, the organizations are names that appear frequently in the media, enabling students to gather new material easily and so providing scope for research and follow-up activities.

Activities

Each unit is supported by a number of activities that help to confirm and extend the student's understanding of the material. These activities will also enable students to appreciate the relationship between the different factors that influence decision-making, and will also provide links with other areas of the syllabus. The activities take various forms:

- Short-answer questions are used to help develop the ability of factual recall and some degree of comprehension and application. They will be valuable in preparing for tests or time-constrained written work.
- The case studies provide the vehicle for a wider application of business skills, the analysis of business situations and the opportunity to make well-informed reference in a variety of written work.
- The local studies provide the context for imaginative and well-directed BTEC National and GNVQ assignments as well as reflecting the particular requirement of the Cambridge Examination Board.
- The media analysis supplies the wider context for business ideas and concepts and will help students to understand organizations within a broader perspective.

Matthew Glew and Michael Watts

Acknowledgements

Every effort has been made to contact the holders of copyright material but if any have been inadvertently overlooked the publishers will be pleased to make the necessary arrangements at the first opportunity.

L = left
R = right
T = top
B = bottom

The publishers would like to thank the following for permission to reproduce photographs:

Our Price Ltd: p. 1;
MFI Furniture Group Plc pp. 9, 10(TR) and 17;
British Airways plc: pp. 23, 24, 25, 27(L and R) and 28;
Body Shop plc: pp. 30, 34(B) and 38(B);
ICL Retail Systems: p. 40;
Peritas Ltd: pp. 42(T) and 45;
Toyota Motor Corporation: pp. 52, 53(L and R), 55, 56, 57(T and B);
J Sainsbury plc: pp. 63(TL, BL, TR and BR) and 69;
Microsoft Corporation: Screen shots © 1992 Microsoft Corporation. All rights reserved. Reprinted with permission from Microsoft Corporation: p 73(R);
Bruce Artwick Organization Ltd: p. 73(L);
TPD Publishing Ltd: p. 73(R).

For permission to reproduce text or information in the form of charts, diagrams, graphs and tables:

Our Price Ltd for illustrations of its various logos (p. 1); for information about the distribution of its stores throughout Britain (p. 2); for details of the organizational structure of the company(p. 7); for information about its advertising policies (p. 8L) and the results of market research on factors affecting the demand for an individual release (p. 8R).

WH Smith Group plc for information on the principal subsidiaries and associated undertakings of WH Smith (p. 6).

MFI Furniture Group Plc for: map showing the distribution of MFI stores throughout Britain (p. 10L); details of the various branches of MFI's manufacturing operations (p. 10R); figures relating to MFI's financial performance, 1985–93 (p. 15) and references to 'MFI Furniture Group Plc Annual Report & Accounts'.

Barclays Bank plc, Economics Department for Interest Rates (p. 12) and Sterling Exchange Rates (p. 19).

The Central Statistical office for information on total consumer expenditure, 1985–92 (pp. 16 and 17).

Financial Times for article 'Recovery hopes dealt double blow', 14 October 1993.

British Airways plc for figures giving numbers of passengers in 1992 (p. 20L); British Airways' Mission and Goals (p. 20R).

Body Shop plc for 'The Body Shop Charter' (p. 30R); 'The Growth of the Body Shop' (p. 31); Creating the right product' (p. 34); leaflet on waste (p. 35); selection of Body Shop leaflets (p. 36) and Body Shop Survey Card (p. 38T).

The Independent for articles, 'The Brighton Beach patrols go for the Burn', 12 July 1993 (p. 37) and 'Roddick libel claim lands a body blow', 31 July 1993 (p. 39).

The National Training Award Office for permission to reproduce their logo (p. 41).

The *Labour Market Quarterly Review*, August 1993, for statistics relating to training (pp. 41–2).

Times Newspapers for an extract from 'Improved practices abound', an article in *The Times*, 4 February 1993. © Michael Hatfield/Times Newspapers Limited 1993.

ICL for 'Four principles of customer care' (p. 47L) and extracts from 'Communicating with people' (p. 47R).

Toyota Motor Corporation for production figures and export figures (p. 51); information on the working of the Toyota production system, pp. 57, 58, 59, 60 and 61.

J Sainsbury plc for information for reference by the author while writing the text to: 'Annual Report and Accounts' 1993; 'A Day in the Life of a Graduate Trainee Accountant'; 'Some Facts about Sainsbury's' and 'A History of Sainsbury's' and reproduction of figures/extracts from these on pp. 64, 67, 68, 69 and 71.

Midland Bank plc for material from the Midland Business Plan, 1994 version (p. 75).

Microsoft Magazine, Volume 3, Issue 4, Spring/Summer 1993 for article, 'Windows for Workgroups strikes chord in peer-to-peer market' (p. 79).

Businesses in the economy

Our Price

1

Introduction

Our Price has a nationwide chain of shops that provide all the latest chart successes, together with a wide range of new releases and back catalogue titles. The music is provided on CDs, cassettes and videos, with vinyl available on order. The shops also sell feature films on video and computer games.

Our Price caters largely for people between the ages of 25 and 35 who have an interest in music. All the shops have the same design and layout and try to create an informal and friendly environment in which the customer can feel at ease. They are served by sales staff who are selected for their genuine interest in music and are therefore capable of providing a helpful and knowledgeable service.

This business strategy used by Our Price has been very successful and it is now the UK's top music retailer.

Products on display in an Our Price store.

Growth and development
The early years

Our Price has achieved its success in a relatively short time. The first shop was opened in 1971 on the Finchley Road in northwest London and traded under the name of 'Tape Revolution'. The shop specialized in the growing market for pre-recorded cassettes. During the first five years of trading the business gradually developed, and by 1976 there were six Tape Revolution shops. However, vinyl records still had a major foothold in the music market and so the business decided to complement its sale of cassettes with records. This required a change of name, and so Our Price Records was born.

By adopting a strategy of strong promotion and highly competitive pricing, the business went from strength to strength. In the spring of 1980 the company acquired the Harlequin chain of record shops. This acquisition, combined with several others, meant that Our Price Records now comprised fifty-seven shops, all based in Southern England.

Expansion in the 1980s

During the 1980s, Our Price Records exploited the market opportunity for a chain of specialist music stores, and as a result it enjoyed a period of spectacular growth and recognition. By 1984 it had become a limited company with seventy-seven outlets. By 1986 the business had 130 shops, and it expanded still further when the company integrated with 'Sound FX' and 'Music Market', and changed its name to Our Price Music to reflect the wider range of music formats being stocked.

1976

1981

1986

1988

The new logo 1993

The growth and development of the company has been reflected in its changing logo.

It was then, in 1986, that Our Price Music was purchased by WH Smith, becoming part of its group of companies. This provided a link with a ready source of retail expertise and experience in the music market. WH Smith Group plc continued to operate Our Price Music as a separate, specialist retailer of recorded music. It believed that Our Price Music's activities in the music market were complementary to those of WH Smith Retail.

A further development was the acquisition of seventy-four Virgin shops in 1988. By the beginning of the 1990s Our Price Music had grown to over 300 shops spread throughout the country. In 1993 Our Price dropped the word 'Music' from its name to reflect the expansion of its product range into videos and games.

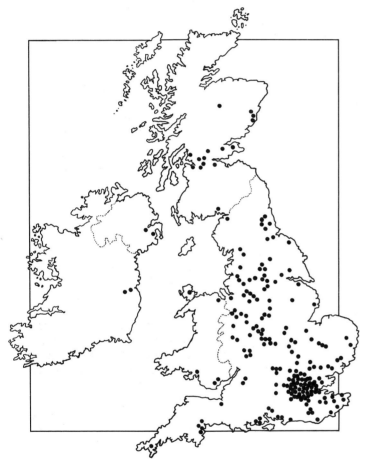

There are over 300 Our Price stores spread throughout the UK.

Approach to the market

Since its early days, Our Price has always worked on the simple market strategy of supplying its customers with exactly what they want. This involves a wide selection of products, sold by knowledgeable staff, providing good service in a well-designed, inviting environment with a convenient high street location.

This strategy has included tailoring the stock in the stores to reflect the musical preferences of a particular region. For example, in the North there is a preference for heavy metal whereas customers in the South-East prefer jazz and soul. Reggae sells well in both London and Bristol.

Our Price has also tried to keep its customers informed about what music is available. In fact the company was the first record retailer to advertise on both radio and television. This is generally carried out through a joint initiative with a record company to coincide with a new release or reissue.

Our Price has also involved itself directly in promoting the music industry. Album signings and personal appearances take place within stores, and support is given to up-and-coming bands.

The general role of businesses in the economy

The rapid growth and development of Our Price and its special relationship with WH Smith Group plc mean that it is large enough and flexible enough to survive in the highly competitive business environment of the 1990s. However, before we go on to analyse its structure and goals, it is important to clarify certain general points about the role of businesses in the modern economy.

Organizations within the modern economy that help to satisfy the needs of individuals

Every individual has to satisfy three types of basic needs: material needs, collective needs and employment needs.

1   **Material needs** refer to items that are felt to be necessary to sustain an individual's expected and accepted standard of living within the community. These items will vary according to a country's relative wealth and stage of development. In all countries, at any stage of development, they would include food, basic clothing and shelter. In a developed economy like the UK they might also include freezers, microwave ovens and fashionable clothing.
2   **Collective needs** cover the economic and social wants of both the individual and the community at large. They include law and order, defence, public and general health facilities, transport and communications, and educational and social services.
3   **Employment needs** – primarily the need to obtain and sustain employment – arise out of the need of individuals to find the resources (a) to meet their own needs, and (b) to support those who are dependent upon them, such as their children, or members of their family who are elderly or sick or who are full-time caregivers.

An individual working alone generally lacks the ability to satisfy all of these needs directly. He or she has to rely on others for help. For example, the individual relies upon people working in factories for the supply of a car, a television, a washing machine or a dishwasher; upon members of the armed forces for defence; upon the police and judiciary for law and order; upon teachers in schools and colleges for education; and upon doctors, nurses and health workers for healthcare. The individual also depends upon factories, offices, shops and other places of work for employment opportunities, and hence for the means of satisfying his or her own material needs.

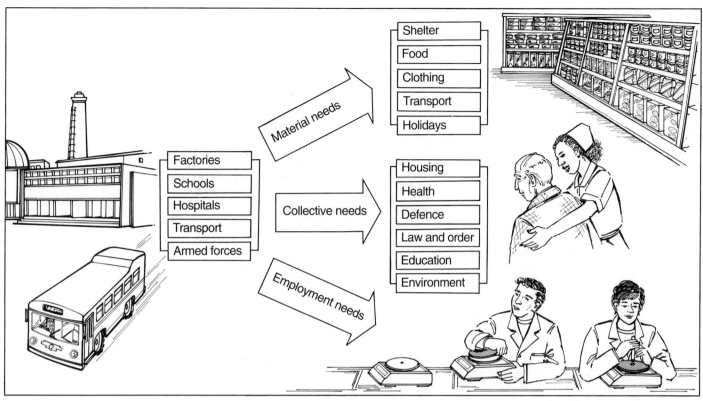

Basic needs

The mixed economy

Within the UK all the organizations that the individual relies upon fall within the mixed economy. This is made up of two sectors: the public and the private. Basically, this means a mixture of organizations that are government controlled and administered together with those that are administered privately. The main types of organization operating within each sector are shown in the illustration below.

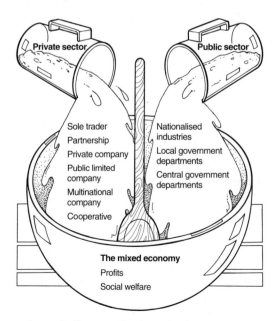

Main types of organization operating in a mixed economy

The public sector

This is controlled by the government and is made up of both business and administrative organizations. The nationalized industries include the Post Office, British Rail and British Coal. They were created by Act of Parliament; they are owned by the general public and controlled by the government.

These industries were originally taken under public control for economic, organizational, strategic or social reasons. However, Conservative governments since 1979 have followed a policy of privatizing these organizations, which has involved transferring them back to the private sector.

Central and local government departments are responsible for helping to satisfy social needs by running and administering government activities and services such as housing, health, education, defence and the environment.

Some confusion exists as to the objectives that should be followed by the organizations in the public sector. They may embrace commercial, economic and social factors. Since the Second World War successive governments have had difficulty in deciding whether public sector organizations should be concerned solely with providing a service in order to maximize welfare, whether they should break even and in doing so cover their costs, or whether they should make a profit and run on commercial lines.

The private sector

This part of the economic system is independent of direct government control. The decision to operate as a sole trader, partnership, private company, public limited company, multinational or cooperative is largely determined by the nature and size of the venture undertaken.

It may be said that businesses in this sector are concerned with maximizing profits, or at least with achieving normal profit. Normal profit is the level of profit sufficient to produce a return on capital that compensates the owners for the risks they have taken. Obviously, the perception of what the level of normal profit is will vary according to the degree of risk within the market – the greater the risk the higher the perceived level of normal profit.

In reality, the owners of private-sector businesses will not be motivated solely by a desire to maximize profits; they may also be influenced by other factors.

Power and control
Some family businesses may limit their expansion, because they do not wish to spread the ownership of the business through the sale of more shares as this could reduce the family's direct power and control over the business.

Proudfoot & Proudfoot Board meeting

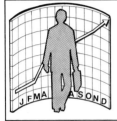

Security
Striving for a higher level of profit may involve a level of risk that the owners feel to be unacceptable. They may consider it a more desirable objective to increase the volume of sales, thus providing a more secure position in the market.

Status and prestige
Very large companies may be motivated by a desire to become larger or to become associated with a new product or revolutionary technique.

INNOVATIONS
Research Breakthrough for Proudfoot & Proudfoot

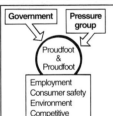

Government   Pressure group
Proudfoot & Proudfoot
Employment
Consumer safety
Environment
Competitive

External influences
Private businesses may respond to pressure from governments and pressure groups on key economic, social, political, legal and environmental issues.

Factors influencing private-sector businesses.

The structure of organizations

The structure of any business stems from its objectives. It represents the network or pattern of relationships between people both as individuals and as members of a working group. Included within this is the way in which people communicate and are coordinated and the methods by which authority and responsibility are exercised by managers, supervisors and employees.

Organizational structures reflect three basic theories: the classical or traditional theory, the behaviourist or human relations theory, and the systems theory.

Classical or traditional
This theory concentrates on the way in which tasks should be grouped under departments or functional areas. There should be clear lines of responsibility, authority should be delegated and derived from the position of the individual in relation to a functional area, and members of the organization should be line-managed by one person.

Behaviourist or human relations
This theory concentrates on how people actually work together. It is based on Professor Elton Mayo's claim that productivity in any organization can be raised by improving human relations. This suggests that organizations need to be structured in a way that encourages consultation between management and the workforce, and that the latter should be able to contribute to decision making.

Systems
This theory emphasizes that organizations are part of a system that takes resources from the environment, converts them into a good or a service, and then puts them back into the environment. It stresses the national interdependence of the systems of various organizations. Each system is made up of a series of sub-systems. Ultimately an organization's system will depend upon its structure, the nature of the workforce, the level of technology employed and its objectives. The effectiveness of the organization's structure will depend upon the sub-systems governing these other factors.

Typically, organizational structures reflect two levels of relationships: the formal structure and the informal structure.

Formal structure
The formal set of relationships reflects the disposition of authority, span of control and chain of command and is often set down in the form of an organization chart. This approach reflects three types of authority.

(a) **Line** authority stems from the ultimate or fundamental authority to command, act or decide on matters affecting others, and to require them to act on any decision made or orders given that are directly concerned with achieving the organization's overall objectives.
(b) **Staff** authority is held by people in an advisory role who give assistance and make recommendations for line managers to act upon.
(c) **Functional** authority is given to specialists in a particular area, who have the right to give orders regarding matters relating to that function.

Informal structure
This reflects the fact that within the working environment a social system exists through people forming social groups and developing informal and often unofficial methods of getting things done. Management may capitalize on this by building it into the decision-making process.

The form of organizational structure is likely to change according to circumstances of the business environment.

A business facing a stable market with a well-established product that is unlikely to be affected by changes in technology would probably adopt a *mechanistic* organizational structure. This would reflect the classical model with precise definitions of employee's tasks and the technical methods to be employed. It would also have a strong vertical system of communication and control, involving line relationships and an emphasis on the importance of loyalty to superiors.

On the other hand, a business facing a rapidly changing environment where modification and improvement are regularly made in the product or service, and where the methods of production or operation are subject to technical change, would be likely to adopt an *organic* organization structure. This would create a situation where jobs are regularly redefined, where there is little specialization and a network system of control, communication and authority. The employees would emphasize the overall objectives of the organization rather than the achievement of a particular task or function.

Size and growth of organizations

Over the last two decades, the ownership of industrial and commercial activities has become markedly more concentrated. The output of many goods and services is now under the control of a few major companies. The motive for such developments is increased profits. This concentration of ownership is often achieved through various forms of integration and expansion.

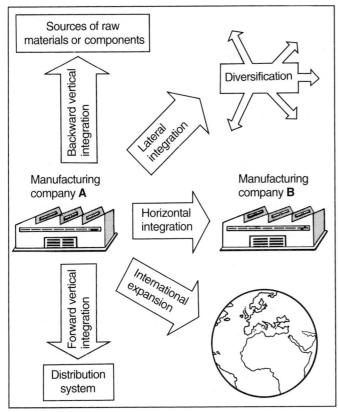

Forms of integration and expansion.

Horizontal integration

A firm may expand horizontally when it increases the scale of its operations while continuing to specialize in its existing range of output. This may be achieved through merger or takeover and is generally motivated by a desire to achieve greater economies of scale, in areas such as marketing, purchasing, finance, human

resources, management or technology. For example, two companies involved in the manufacture of electrical consumer goods may choose to merge their operations in order to achieve a larger market share, associated economies of scale, reduction in unit costs and increase in profitability.

Vertical integration

A firm may expand vertically in order to involve itself in additional stages of production or distribution. For example, a company involved in the manufacture of electrical consumer goods may expand vertically backwards by securing its own component manufacturing operation. It may also expand vertically towards the market by securing its own chain of retail outlets.

The major motivation behind vertical integration is to achieve greater control over the whole productive operation and in so doing increase security of supplies, control of the market, efficiency, economies of scale and profitability.

Lateral integration or diversification

A firm may decide to spread its risks across a wider range of products or services by moving into new areas of operation. For example, a tour operator may diversify into hotels or nightclubs.

International expansion

A firm's expansion plans may go beyond its home market and it may seek to expand its sales into overseas markets. In particular this may be the case when the domestic market shows a lack of sustained growth or is experiencing a prolonged recession. This has led to the development of the multinational company and ultimately to the global factory where the firm locates its operation to take advantage of low wage costs, the availability of cheaper supplies of raw materials and components, a favourable economic and political business environment, and the proximity of a strong market.

Our Price's position in the economy – its structure and goals
Satisfaction of needs

Our Price helps to satisfy the material and employment needs of individuals within the UK economy.

Essentially it meets the increasing material demand for goods in the home entertainment music market. This has been brought about by the growth in leisure time, the developing youth culture, the higher levels of disposable income and the influence of technology on music formats.

Our Price attempts to meet these needs by offering a range of music formats and titles and a style of customer service that closely match the characteristics and needs of the local market. This has proved to be successful, and between 1991 and 1992 – when Britain was in the depths of recession – Our Price managed to increase its total sales by 2 per cent in value. Within this increase its sales moved towards compact discs, which accounted for 43 per cent of sales. Vinyl accounted for 4 per cent of sales, as compared to 11 per cent in 1990/1. Video sales increased by 5 per cent.

Our Price contributes to the satisfaction of employment needs at two levels. At the beginning of the 1990s it *directly* employed some 2,000 people, mostly on a full-time basis. Each store is under a manager, aided by an assistant and a number of sales staff. Managerial and executive appointments are generally made from within the company. This policy obviously helps to encourage commitment, motivation and staff development at all levels. It means that a young person who joins the company as a shop assistant can aspire towards a managerial position, thus satisfying both their immediate and long-term employment needs.

Our Price also contributes *indirectly* to the satisfaction of employment needs by creating a market for the services and products of other organizations, while also drawing upon the various public and private sector services for running its own business. In so doing it helps to satisfy the employment needs of people seeking work as distributors, artists, writers, producers, manufacturers, designers, publishers and shop fitters, in the communications, energy and transport industries, and in government administration.

Position within the mixed economy

Our Price Limited operates within the private sector as a subsidiary of WH Smith Group plc. The Group is made up of a number of principal subsidiaries and associated undertakings as shown in the following table.

Name	Activity	Class of share	Effective Group interest (%)
Principal subsidiaries *Held directly* WH Smith Limited	Retailing Distribution	Ordinary	100.0
WH Smith Office Supplies Limited	Distribution	Ordinary	100.0
Held indirectly Our Price Music Limited	Retailing	Ordinary	100.0
Waterstone Investments Limited	Retailing	Ordinary	81.6
WH Smith Group (USA) Inc	Retailing	Common	100.0
Pentagon Group Limited	Distribution	Ordinary	100.0
Satex Group PLC	Distribution	Ordinary	100.0
Sandhurst Marketing PLC	Distribution	Ordinary	100.0
Cartwright Brice Holdings Limited	Distribution	Ordinary	100.0
H J Chapman & Company Limited	Distribution	Ordinary	100.0
Principal Associated undertakings *Held indirectly*	Distribution	Ordinary	100.0
Do It All Limited	Do it yourself	Ordinary	50.0
Virgin Retail Limited	Retailing	Ordinary	50.0
With the exception of WH Smith Group (USA) Inc, which is incorporated and operates in the United States of America, the principal subsidiaries and associated undertakings are registered in England and operate in the United Kingdom.			

WH Smith Group plc – principal subsidiaries and associated untertakings.

The Group exercises direct control over the business policies and activities of its parent operations of WH Smith Limited and WH Smith Office Supplies Limited. It exercises indirect control over its other subsidiaries. Therefore Our Price Limited, as one of the businesses making up WH Smith Group, is allowed its own distinctive brand, its own clearly defined market segment and its own way of conducting business. Do It All Limited represents a joint venture with Boots, and similarly it shares the ownership of Virgin Retail Limited with the Virgin Group.

The Group considers that its major goal is to provide the products that the customer wants, making them available when they need them, and at the right price. To achieve this the Group attempts to ensure that the market share is effectively managed, that capital is allocated to achieve the best long-term returns and that there is a coordinated business strategy across the Group.

Throughout the group of companies there is considerable expertise in customer care, warehousing and distribution, and buying and marketing systems. Consequently there is considerable potential to achieve economies of scale by developing an integrated distribution system to cover all the retail businesses.

Potential economies also exist in the handling of property in terms of acquiring new sites and extending or remodelling existing outlets.

The cost advantages associated with these economies give the Group an extensive competitive advantage in the retailing and distribution of books, newspapers, stationery, recorded music, video and computer games.

Our Price's objectives

Our Price's objectives clearly reflect the principal objective of all private sector organizations – to maximize profits. They also embrace WH Smith Group plc's overall coordinated business strategy. This gives an additional focus in that it provides Our Price with a more secure market position. There is also a Group desire to achieve the status of leading retailer of music products.

Within the WH Smith Group's overall coordinated business strategy, Our Price was given a position between the specialist (Virgin) and the generalist (WH Smith). Its focus is on providing customers with a range of predominantly new products that are easy to find and competitively priced. Our Price recognized that in order to achieve this it is essential that everybody within the company shares the same values. This means that all employees should treat the customers in a way that reflects company values. It also means that every member of staff must recognize the importance of customer satisfaction, and appreciate the retail and commercial disciplines that underpin future performance. At the same time, the company is committed to empowering staff to make decisions.

Our Price's objectives are also influenced by certain external factors and pressures. WH Smith Group plc is involved in a number of community issues, sponsoring the arts, education and improvements in literacy. It has also responded to external pressures to create a greener environment. In 1991 the Group issued a statement of intent on the environment. During 1992, the Group began to implement this statement, giving particular attention to the products it sells and its use of energy and materials. More specifically, Our Price Music started to reduce the size of its carrier bags and make them from recycled waste, and to produce all of its forms on recycled paper.

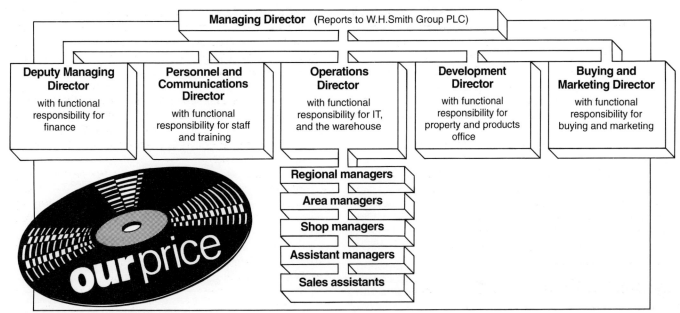

The organizational structure of Our Price.

Organizational structure

The formal organizational structure of Our Price is shown in the diagram above.

All the businesses making up WH Smith Group plc are allowed to operate independently. However, the managing director of Our Price reports directly to the main board and has to ensure that the Group's overall goals and coordinating strategies are incorporated within the company's policies.

The five directors making up the board have functional responsibility for certain key areas throughout the company. The deputy managing director is expected to deputize formally for the managing director when necessary.

The operations director line-manages the whole of the distribution process through three regional managers, who in turn line-manage a group of area managers, who take responsibility for a number of shop managers.

Within each shop the manager works very closely with his or her assistant. Managers and assistants are encouraged to develop a close partnership as many of the tasks they perform overlap. The shop managers have considerable autonomy over the music products they stock. All managers have a core stock list that acts as a guide, but they are encouraged to order anything that they think will sell. Delegating responsibility in this way enables each shop to have the benefits that an independent music retailer would have, while still being supported by the resources of a strong multiple operation. Shop assistants are encouraged to acquire as much working and product knowledge as possible and then to aspire towards a management position.

Very good lines of communication exist throughout the structure, and consultation with staff is encouraged. The managing director talks directly to all staff through the in-house company newsletter, entitled 'Our Price Our Company'.

Empowering the staff at shop level to make decisions helps to develop many of the informal structures and relationships that are necessary for the success of a company's operations.

Our Price's organizational structure reflects some elements of a classical approach, in that tasks are clearly grouped under particular functional areas and the distribution process is line-managed from the operations director downwards. However, the company prides itself on its approach to human relations and on the willingness of management to consult with the workforce and delegate authority.

Activities

Short-answer questions

1   Identify the factors that have contributed to the rapid growth of Our Price and its success in the music market.
2   Suggest the ways in which central and local government services might provide help for Our Price, in terms of locating its shops, protecting its stock, and ensuring the safety of its customers.
3   List the potential economies of scale associated with the retailing of music products.
4   Considering Our Price's objectives do you feel that the company should consider opening shops in Europe and America?
5   How far does the organizational structure of Our Price allow for the development and adoption of new ideas? Justify your answer.
6   Identify and comment upon Our Price's position within the market.
7   How does Our Price attempt to motivate its staff?
8   Give two examples of how Our Price has integrated horizontally, and suggest the business advantages that have arisen out of these specific cases.
9   What was the motive behind WH Smith Group plc's decision to acquire Our Price?
10 To what extent has Our Price diversified its activities and in so doing secured its position for the future?

Case study

The extract over the page has been taken from the Our Price's Newsletter for May 1993:

our advertising

'Bombs not Bullets' was the phrase that resulted from a meeting between Phil Webb, the Our Price Ad Manager, and the new advertising agency WCRS. The point is to develop a fresh and innovative new concept for Our Price, which hits the target audience with a bang – a major, large scale and dynamic ad strategy, rather than minor, more frequent campaigns.

'We need to build on the current Our Price image, but create a strong brand identity and attitude which will lead the way in music retailing advertising. Our Price needs to develop a specific personality which will be instantly recognisable by all present and potential customers. The concept must be ageless and reflect our brand values of Currency, Price and Convenience,' says Phil.

'Ballsy but Cheeky' was WCRS's reply and so was the ideas they came up with.

The Brit Awards were the first ads created by WCRS for Our Price and caused considerable excitement in the trade for the mould-breaking application. Featuring Brit Eckland describing in her own breathless tones her suggested nomination for the Brit awards whilst also promoting the Our Price Brits special offer.

These ads showed a total change of tack from the usual music advertising of a video or promo sandwiched between the branded message. It was also the birth of the new Our Price humorous play on words and the development of a specific persona and attitude.

At this time Our Price also introduced the new strap line 'YOUR CHOICE OUR PRICE' which will run in all advertising for an indefinite period.

These TV ads were quickly followed by the innovative 'SIMPLY REDuced' 48-sheet posters which were pasted around the country and used to promote the Warners offer. The ads and the promotion were phenomenally successful both in and outside the industry. Our Price believes this is the first time that a major band has spearheaded a retailer's promotion in such a bold way.

'In future we plan that all ads on the TV and in the national press will include a simple price message (which is after all what our customers want to hear), communicated through a bigger and bolder image but with the added benefit of a fine and subtle humour which we believe will bring a wry smile to even the most hardened customer's lips,' says Phil.

From June Our Price will be investing more into event-driven campaigns which will correspond to topical promotions ongoing throughout our product range – including videos and games so . . . watch this space for more wild ideas, fun and games from Phil and his Ad team!

1   What is the value to the consumer of the approach to advertising described in the extract?
2   Our Price operates in a highly competitive market environment. To what extent does this justify the amount the company spends on advertising?
3   Imagine that Our Price were operating in a more centrally controlled economy. Why would its advertising budget probably be less? How would its advertising message change? Explain your answers.

Local investigation

1   Our Price's market research department has identified the following factors as being important in determining the demand for an individual release.

Factor	Effect
Discount offered	Will affect where customers buy from but will not strongly affect the total demand for a current title. Can radically alter the sales patterns of older titles however.
Airplay	Very powerful.
Television	Extremely powerful.
Advertising	Depends on frequency, timing and effectiveness of ad.
Artist loyalty	Strong fan-based albums will normally sell very strongly in the first couple of weeks – this will affect how many copies we will decide to stock initially.
Fashion	Will only have strong effect if allied with one of the above.
Discos	Dance singles can enter the Charts very high if they are given exposure in clubs. This will not really impact album sales.
Disposable income	With older titles, price can be a factor, which is why many are reduced to 'mid-price' or 'budget-price' by record companies.
Numbers of people in different age groups	This is borne in mind when doing long-term planning where changes in demographics may affect our commitment to different formats.
Ownership of audio equipment	The 'penetration' of different types of audio equipment into the marketplace clearly has an effect on the quantities of different formats that we will stock.
Seasonality	Only Christmas really has any impact.
Music press	Generally only has a strong effect if allied with TV or radio exposure.
Word of mouth	Strong sales can still be achieved by an artist building a solid live reputation.

Factors affecting demand for an individual release.

(a) Select three titles from the current top ten in the charts and identify which of these factors were most significant in putting the record into that position. By reference to the music press justify your suggestions.
(b) Arrange an interview with the Manager of your local Our Price store and ask him or her to rank the demand factors for the local area.
(c) From your findings in (a) and (b) comment on the type of material needs satisfied by Our Price's products and the standard of living represented both locally and nationally.

2   (a) Visit your nearest WH Smith and Our Price stores.
(b) Compare the types of music products sold in the two stores and identify the target markets they are aimed at. Analyse the extent to which this reflects the fact that the two retailers are satisfying different material wants for different groups.
(c) Identify any common business strategies operating within the two establishments.

The business environment
MFI Furniture Group

2

Introduction

MFI is the leading furniture retailer in the UK. It also owns one of the largest furniture manufacturing operations in Europe. The company has about 11.4 per cent, by value, of the UK market for household furniture, and it is estimated that this is over two and a half times the market share of its nearest competitor. MFI's market share is greatest in its core market sectors: self-assembly kitchens and bedroom furniture. Each of these accounts for about 30 per cent of MFI's retail sales in the UK.

Growth and development

Early expansion

Mullard Furniture Industries started out as a mail-order business in the mid-1960s. It was one of the pioneers of the UK market for self-assembly furniture. In the mid-1970s the mail order business gave way to a cash-and-carry retail operation. MFI created one of the UK's first chains of edge-of-town superstores and this chain was then expanded by the takeover of Status Discount Ltd, a major competitor.

By the early 1980s MFI had developed close relationships with its main suppliers, especially Humber Kitchens Ltd, a specialist manufacturer of self-assembly furniture. In 1982 the company also took its first major step in product branding with the acquisition – jointly with Humber Kitchens – of the Hygena brand name, which Humber Kitchens then used as its own trading name.

Management buyout

MFI was acquired by Associated Dairies Group plc (ASDA) in 1985, but in 1987 MFI was bought out by a group of seven directors, some 350 managers and a number of financial institutions investing money on behalf of their savers. The buyout was backed by a syndicate of banks. Although the purchase included a share in the Hygena brand name, the buyout team went further and, to safeguard MFI's supply of an important range of products, bought the Hygena company itself.

Further expansion

The strategy of the new management team was to expand MFI's product range, improve quality and customer service, introduce new superstore formats and continue with the development of the superstore network. Expansion into new and higher quality products was achieved by introducing new brands. In 1988, for example, MFI acquired Schreiber, which had a well-established reputation for kitchen and bedroom furniture, and this allowed MFI to appeal to an older and more up-market customer. Expansion based upon this kind of vertical integration has been a vital aspect of MFI's growth strategy. In July 1992 MFI was floated on the stock exchange.

With Hygena, MFI acquired a retail business in France called Hygena Cuisines. By 1993 there were forty-one outlets made up of main stores, satellite boutiques and smaller shops located in shopping centres. All of these are linked to the MFI computer system and supply chain, and about 80 per cent of the products that MFI sells in France are sourced in the UK.

A packed and bar-coded Hygena product at MFI's manufacturing base at Howden, North Humberside.

In 1993 MFI had 176 superstores, mainly in edge-of-town locations, and five High-Street shops, providing good geographic coverage of the UK. The company continually seeks to identify locations for new superstores as well as new locations for some of its existing stores. Research is also undertaken to establish the most effective store format for displaying products, and the new layouts and designs are then gradually introduced into existing stores.

MFI's Hygena and Schreiber product brands are the best recognized furniture brands in the UK in their respective sectors. In

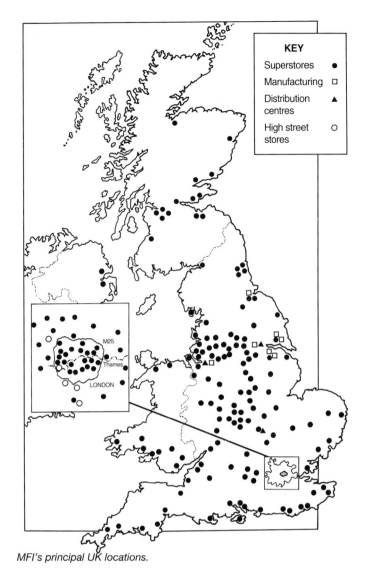

KEY

Superstores	●
Manufacturing	□
Distribution centres	▲
High street stores	○

MFI's principal UK locations.

MFI Huddersfield, one of the ten stores refitted during 1992.

self-assembly kitchens MFI's estimated market share by volume is over two and a half the estimated share of its nearest rival, B&Q, and in self-assembly bedrooms its estimated market share by volume is over four times the estimated share of its nearest rival, in this case Texas. It is also the clear market leader by volume in rigid kitchens, a major retailer of beds and the largest seller of AEG built-in kitchen appliances.

Approach to the market

Branding and market segmentation are important features of MFI's marketing strategy, which has allowed the company to widen its appeal without losing its core customers. MFI's customer profile closely matches that of UK furniture buyers as a whole. Hygena buyers, for example, are mainly middle-income families, while Schreiber purchasers are generally more affluent. Other product brands developed in recent years are Greaves and Thomas for upholstery and dining room furniture, Deltek for home office furniture, Ashton Dean for coordinated textiles, and Pronto, which has allowed MFI to develop its traditional cash-and-carry business.

MFI manufactures products in-house only when the production process is capable of significant automation and where there are likely to be high volume sales and a rapid return on investment. Potential sales are assessed using a combination of

market research and the test marketing of bought-in products. About 60 per cent of the value of MFI's sales are sourced internally. Its manufacturing facilities are listed in the following table.

Company	Site	Production area (sq. ft.)	Principal products
Hygena	Howden	579,000	Cabinets
	Hull	92,000	Solid timber doors
	Scunthorpe	283,000	Solid and veneered timber doors
	Stockton-on-Tees	368,000	PVC doors, laminated doors, drawer boxes, drawer runners, sinks and hobs
Greens	Hull	249,000	Panels, components, small cabinets, fittings, handle packs, plastic products and vacuum formed doors for bedroom cabinets
Schreiber	Runcorn	374,000	Cabinets and doors
Hygena Packaging	Scunthorpe	175,000	Printed corrugated board and cartons
		2,120,000	

MFI's manufacturing operations.

The main raw materials used in these manufacturing operations include chipboard, fibreboard, solid wood, veneers, paper for producing laminated surfaces, and door components. These materials are readily available and are sourced from a range of suppliers around the world. Finished products sourced externally include textiles, upholstery, beds, home office furniture and dining furniture, some fitted kitchen appliances, most sinks and some kitchen and bedroom doors.

Purchases are concentrated on individual suppliers, to give MFI more influence over price and quality and to simplify buying, ordering and delivery. In some cases suppliers are linked to MFI's computer systems so that orders can be processed automatically. No external supplier of finished products accounts for more than 3.5 per cent of MFI's sales. Overall, including in-house manufacture, 86 per cent of the products supplied to its stores are manufactured in the UK. The other 14 per cent come mainly from Europe.

Developments in the economic and financial environment

Like many companies that have to survive in a highly competitive market, MFI must always pay strict attention to the need to offer value for money to households in the market segments where it operates. Any complacency about such matters as its pricing strategy, product range, quality, customer services, the location and format of its stores and the training and development of its employees will soon show itself in the company's financial performance and market share. However, despite the resources that MFI continually devotes to strengthening its competitive position, it is part of an industry whose prospects are greatly influenced by developments in the economic and financial aspects of the business environment. In this respect the government plays a major role in creating the trading environment in which MFI operates. This is because it has the power to change interest rates and taxes, and to follow policies that influence other important areas affecting MFI, such as the housing market and consumer confidence.

Companies must take several factors into account when seeking to predict short-term and medium-term developments in their markets. Perhaps the most important factor is government intervention that seeks to manipulate the total level of consumer spending. Forecasting is made more difficult by the fact that the nature, extent and timing of such government intervention is itself very difficult to predict. Such intervention is usually aimed at trying to deal with inflation or persistently high unemployment.

The effects of anti-inflationary measures upon the business environment

If total spending in the economy rises faster than the rate at which the total output of goods and services can be increased, then this will eventually lead to inflation (i.e. rising prices). The kinds of developments that lead to the creation of a wage–price spiral are shown in the diagram below.

To tackle inflation, the government will seek to depress the level of total spending in the economy, and in seeking to achieve this objective it can select from a range of economic measures.

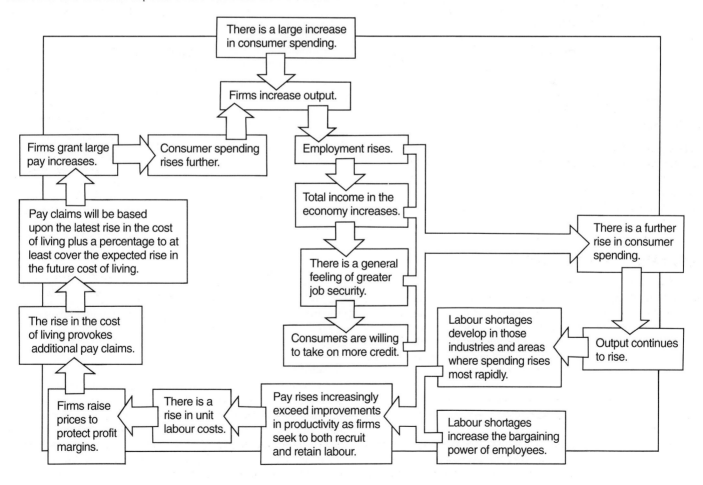

The wage–price spiral.

A rise in interest rates

Higher rates of interest will increase the costs of borrowing and this will affect companies in several ways:

1   There will be an increase in the interest charges that companies have to pay on their existing borrowing, for example in the form of loans or overdrafts from banks. To finance this increase in costs, companies will have to look for ways of making savings in other areas. Since labour generally accounts for the largest proportion of costs, they will seek to introduce changes in working practices that allow them to meet their market demand with a reduced workforce. Companies will therefore make some employees redundant and take a firmer stand against excessive pay claims.

Date	Rate	Date	Rate	Date	Rate
1986		1988 (cont.)		1991 (cont.)	
Jan 9	12.5	Apr 11	8	Feb 27	13
Mar 19	11.5	May 18	7.5	Mar 22	12.5
Apr 8	11	Jun 3	8	Apr 12	12
Apr 21	10.5	Jun 6	8.5	May 24	11.5
May 27	10	Jun 22	9	Jul 12	11
Oct 14	11	Jun 28	9.5	Sep 4	10.5
1987		Jul 4	10	1992	
Mar 10	10.5	Jul 18	10.5	May 5	10
Mar 18	10	Aug 8	11	Sep 16	12
Apr 29	9.5	Aug 25	12	Sep 18	10
May 11	9	Nov 25	13	Sep 22	9
Aug 7	10	1989		Oct 16	8
Oct 26	9.5	May 24	14	Nov 13	7
Nov 5	9	Oct 5	15	1993	
Dec 4	8.5	1990		Jan 26	6
1988		Oct 8	14	Nov 23	5.5
Feb 2	9	1991		1994	
Mar 17	8.5	Feb 13	13.5	Feb 8	5.25

Barclays Banks base rates. The government can use changes in interest rates to influence the level of consumer spending.
Source: Barclays Quarterly Review, Second Quarter 1994.

2   Higher interest rates will also make it more expensive to raise loan capital needed to finance capital investment projects. Modernization and expansion programmes will therefore be postponed or scaled down. Companies may also cut investment expenditure in order to make money available both to reduce their existing borrowing and to help meet the interest charges on remaining debt.
3   The main aim of this policy, however, is to make households pay higher rates of interest on any loans, overdrafts or other forms of credit. The effect will be particularly severe upon households with mortgages, because of the large amounts that may have been borrowed. To help meet higher interest payments many households will have to cut back in other areas of spending. Households will also reduce their take-up of new consumer credit. Companies will therefore face a fall in the demand for their goods and services and this will reduce sales revenue and profits.
4   Future investment projects will also be cut back. This is because the depressed state of the market means a fall in the level of business confidence, and lower profits also mean less money available to finance such projects. Thus an unfortunate side effect of measures aimed at reducing consumer spending is the creation of an environment that damages investment.
5   As well as *charging* higher rates of interest, banks and other lenders will also be *paying* higher rates of interest to those who deposit money with them. Thus financial institutions in the UK that receive deposits will be offering depositors more attractive rates of interest than those offered by similar institutions abroad. The UK will therefore become an attractive place for overseas investors. As these investors exchange their own currencies to buy the pounds that they wish to place on deposit in the UK, so the demand for sterling on foreign exchange markets will increase. This increased demand will raise the price of sterling in relation to foreign currencies – i.e. the exchange rate will rise. The more expensive pound will make UK goods and services more expensive to foreigners, and UK companies will become less competitive than foreign producers. It will also mean that people in the UK will find some foreign goods and services on offer better value for money than those produced in the UK. In summary, a rise in interest rates will push up the exchange rate, and UK companies may lose sales because of lower export orders and higher imports as foreign companies increase their penetration of the UK market.

A rise in income tax

Higher rates of income tax will reduce the average level of disposable income, i.e. the income that remains after tax and national insurance contributions have been deducted. Households will therefore have less money to spend, but the effect upon companies will depend upon what kinds of goods or services they produce.

1   Households are most likely to cut back in the areas they regard as inessential, such as replacing electrical appliances and other consumer durables. Other kinds of consumer spending, such as that on food, may be maintained, although people may switch from the more expensive items to cheaper alternatives.
2   Some goods and services are not affected by the fall in spending power because many people buy them out of habit. They include not only the obvious items like tobacco and alcoholic drinks but also some favoured brands of soft drinks and confectionery, which people may continue to buy regularly without feeling extravagant.
3   Consumer spending on certain goods and services associated with sports, hobbies and other interests may also hold up relatively well because some households may see them as a very important part of their leisure time.

Reducing the value of tax allowances

The government can increase the proportion of income that the average household pays in income tax without actually raising income tax rates. Like most taxes, higher income tax is politically unpopular. Public reaction can be reduced to some extent, however, by a subtler and more indirect way of raising tax revenue and hence reducing consumer spending: by freezing personal tax allowances or not raising them in line with the rate of inflation.

Income tax

Rates	%	1993/4	1992/3
Lower	20	Up to £2,500	Up to £2,000
Basic	25	£2,501 to £23,700	£2,001 to £23,700
Higher	40	Above £23,700	Above £23,700

Allowances	1993/4 (£)	1992/3 (£)
Personal allowance	3,445	3,445
Married couple's allowance	1,720	1,720
Age allowance (65 to 74)		
Personal allowance	4,200	4,200
Married couple's allowance	2,465	2,465
Age allowance (75 or over)		
Personal allowance	4,370	4,370
Married couple's allowance	2,505	2,505
Income limit for age allowance	14,200	14,200

The government can use changes in tax rates, tax bands and allowances to influence the level of consumer spending.

Assume, for example, that the current personal tax allowance is £3,500 and the rate of inflation is 5 per cent. In order to maintain the real purchasing power of this tax-free income the personal allowance should be raised to £3,675. If this allowance is frozen, or raised by less than the rate of inflation, the real value of the allowance will drop, which will in turn affect the level of consumer spending. A similar effect would be achieved if the married couple's allowance were not raised in line with inflation.

Tax bands

Tax bands are the levels of income at which taxpayers become liable to the next rate of income tax. The position as it was in the tax year 1992/93 is shown in the table above. At Budget time the Chancellor of the Exchequer generally increases these tax bands in line with inflation to help protect households from the resulting rise in the cost of living. In some years, however, in order to depress the level of consumer spending, tax bands may be frozen or not raised in line with inflation. Assume, for example, that someone is on an income that is just below the level at which the higher rate of tax comes into operation. This person then receives a pay increase of 5 per cent and this is just sufficient to compensate for the general rise in the cost of living. The Chancellor may raise personal tax allowances and the income band taxed at 20 per cent by 5 per cent but not increase the band of income on which the basic rate of 25 per cent is paid. In our example, therefore, the person receiving the pay rise will find that nearly all of their extra pay is taxed at the higher rate and their disposable income now rises by less than the rise in the cost of living. Because their disposable income now buys less than before, they will be obliged to trim their spending in certain areas.

A rise in VAT

A higher rate of VAT will mean higher prices and hence a lower average level of real disposable income, i.e. the actual purchasing power of disposable income in terms of the quantity of goods and services it will buy. Assume, for example, that an item is priced at £2.35 and that this includes VAT at 17.5 per cent. The rate is then increased to 20 per cent and this item will now be priced at £2.40. This represents a very small price rise and on its own is unlikely to produce a significant fall in the demand for this particular item. The effect of a rise in VAT comes, in fact, from the cumulative effect of increased prices on all the goods and services that are subject to the tax. Every time a household buys a good or service that now carries a higher rate of VAT it has less money left to buy other items, and eventually cuts must be made somewhere. If, for example, a household spends on average £352 a month on items that carry VAT then about £52 of this is accounted for by the tax. A rise in VAT to 20 per cent will mean the total tax on these items now amounts to £60 and a spending of £352 will no longer buy the same amount of goods and services. This household therefore will have to make cut-backs in certain areas unless they are prepared to draw upon their savings to maintain the level of their consumption.

The government can also reduce people's spending power by extending VAT to goods and services that currently do not carry such tax, or introduce different VAT bands for various categories of goods and services. For example, the government may be concerned about the effect of a higher VAT upon the lower income groups and therefore it could choose to introduce a much higher rate that applied only to the kinds of goods and services that tend to be bought by the higher income groups. Similarly those goods and services that are regarded by the majority of households as being exceptionally luxurious could be subject to an even higher VAT band.

A rise in excise duties

Excise duties are the taxes paid on tobacco, alcohol and petrol, and they generally account for a large part of the prices of those goods. The demand for these items is not sensitive to the higher prices caused by higher excise duties. Consumers will find the money to pay higher prices by cutting back on their spending in other areas where they feel they are most able to make savings.

Beer	24.9p per pint
Wine	£1.11½ per 75 cl bottle
Spirits	£5.55 per 70 cl bottle
Tobacco	£1.56 per packet of 20 king size cigarettes
Leaded petrol (4 star)	33.6p per litre
Unleaded petrol	28.7p per litre
Diesel fuel	28.2p per litre
Note: VAT is charged in the final selling price of these goods.	

Level of excise duties excluding VAT (from 1 April 1994)

Cuts in public expenditure

Government spending accounts for about 40 to 45 per cent of all spending in the economy. If the government wishes to reduce the inflationary pressures caused by an excessive increase in total spending then it always has the option of making cuts in some of its spending plans. The government will have to weigh up the likely political, social and economic effects of any such cuts before deciding which departmental budgets will bear the burden of the necessary adjustment. For example, if the government decides to make cuts in spending on defence, then industries linked to defence contracts, such as those in aerospace, electronics, armaments and shipbuilding, will receive fewer orders. Companies in these industries are likely to respond by making some of their workforce redundant and perhaps also cutting back on some of their own capital projects because of the effect upon profits and the decline in the general level of business confidence. Those who lose their jobs will obviously experience a marked fall in their spending. They may be joined by others who are made redundant when suppliers to these main industries experience the knock-on effect of cuts in defence spending.

Bear in mind that the total level of demand in the economy can be reduced, even if the government spends more money than in the previous year. It is the *real* value of government spending that is important. If, for example, the rate of inflation is 4 per cent and the money value of government spending is allowed to rise by 1.5 per cent, then the new level of spending will buy fewer goods and services than before and suppliers will again experience a decline in their business.

Assuming that public sector employees negotiate an average pay rise of 4 per cent, then the new level of public expenditure means that central and local departments cannot afford to employ the same number of people. They may therefore be obliged to make some employees redundant and the households affected will experience a large fall in their spending power.

The government can also hold down pay rises in the public sector, both by controlling pay in central government departments and by limiting or even freezing the grants that it makes to local authorities. Faced with such a situation local authorities will need to negotiate much lower pay settlements with their employees and these are likely to be below the rate of inflation. The result is that many people employed in the public sector will experience a fall in their real spending power and so cut back on certain kinds of spending.

The effect of falling demand upon the business environment

The changes in interest rates, taxes and government spending described above will all contribute to a fall in total demand in the economy. The fall in consumer spending, cuts in capital projects, reductions in government spending, lost export orders and increased imports all lead to a fall in total output in the economy and therefore to rising unemployment. As the economy moves into recession those people still in work will be increasingly concerned about the growing number of redundancies and the constant reference to the depressed state of the economy in the media. These households will feel that their own jobs may soon be under threat, and this sense of insecurity will cause them to change their spending patterns. For example, they may postpone major expenditure on consumer durables and reduce their take up of new credit. Instead they are likely to save more of their income to cushion themselves against the effects of possible unemployment. The decision to save more will also be encouraged by the general rise in interest rates. Thus the initial rise in unemployment produced by government economic policy will create an environment that depresses the·level of consumer confidence among those still in work.

As the level of unemployment rises this will lead to lower pay settlements as employers will be in a much stronger position when negotiating increases with employees. This is a major factor in reducing the rate of increase of unit labour costs and hence the rate of inflation. Depressed markets also mean that producers must make every effort to avoid a rise in costs, particularly labour costs, because they must compete more strongly on prices to protect their sales.

The effect of employment-creating policies upon the business environment

As well as periods of excessive spending in the economy, and the need to reduce inflation, there will be periods when the main problem is one of rising unemployment. These periods occur when total spending in the economy leads to a level of output that does not create enough job opportunities for those available for work. As described earlier, this may partly be the result of policies introduced in a previous period to tackle inflation. The government, having got inflation down to an acceptable level, may therefore be under severe political pressure to deal with an economy that may have slid into a serious recession, with falling output and large-scale redundancies.

The UK may also suffer from unemployment because of developments in the world economy. Countries such as Germany, the United States and France, for example, are important export markets for UK companies and they may all experience a downturn in their own economies. As spending falls in these countries they will reduce imports from the UK and other economies, and as export orders fall the recession will deepen and spread to other parts of the world.

The effect upon MFI of policies to reduce unemployment

The government can try to combat growing unemployment by stimulating total spending in the economy. This will encourage companies to increase output and take on more workers. As employment rises this will raise the purchasing power of more households and yet more jobs will be created. In order to expand demand in the economy the government can reverse the kinds of economic measures used to deal with inflation: for example, it can reduce interest rates, lower income tax, raise tax allowances by more than inflation and increase government spending.

In 1986, unemployment in the UK had reached nearly 3.2 million and to avoid any further rise in the jobless total the government began the process of stimulating total demand in the economy. As the following graph shows, this soon brought about a fall in unemployment. Cuts in interest rates were a major part of the policy and this reduction in the price of credit also occurred at a time when financial institutions were free from regulations that had previously exerted some form of control over their lending activities.

Along with cuts in both the standard and higher rates of income tax, this plentiful and cheap supply of credit led to a dramatic rise in the level of consumer spending. MFI and other companies involved in the manufacture and retailing of furniture, as well as those supplying soft-furnishing products and DIY goods, experienced a rapid rise in the demand for their products. Households used the cheap credit and higher disposable incomes to improve their homes.

As mortgages became cheaper, this period also saw the beginnings of a boom in the housing market, and this created significant market opportunities for MFI:

1 Many existing home owners saw moving home as a good time to replace some of their furnishings.
2 Property was seen increasingly as a safe and valuable investment as it was widely agreed that house prices would continue to rise. Some people therefore moved home on a regular basis as they worked their way up the housing ladder, and this again helped furniture sales.
3 As house prices accelerated, this further fuelled the demand for property. First-time buyers were keen to buy before prices rose even further and this increase in home ownership added to the demand for a wide range of furniture.
4 The willingness of households to take on more credit to refurnish their existing or new home was also encouraged by feelings of greater job security, an increase in job opportunities, and expectations of large pay rises. These had all come about because the consumer spending boom had fuelled an increase in production, and hence a demand for labour. Some companies were facing labour shortages and were continually advertising vacancies, as well as granting pay rises that helped to retain their existing employees.
5 The house price boom also affected the level of consumer credit. Financial institutions were more generous with the amounts they lent to home owners, as well as with the length of the repayment periods offered, because borrowers could offer their homes as security.
6 Owning a house that was rising in price also made consumers more confident in taking on more consumer credit.

The house price boom originated in the South-East and, as the following table shows, it then spread to other parts of the UK.

By 1988 the consumer spending boom was well under way, and MFI took full advantage of the much improved market opportunities. The effects upon MFI are summarized in the table below, where the funds allocated to capital investment and the growth in the workforce also indicate the general improvement in the level of business confidence. Between November 1987 and April 1989 MFI opened twenty-seven new stores and relocated ten others to more favourable sites.

The response of MFI to the rising demand

The buoyant market demand encouraged MFI to carry on with its strategy of expanding into new and higher quality product areas with well-established brand names that would appeal to those on rising incomes. This was the major reason behind its acquisition of Schreiber in 1988.

To take full advantage of the greater feeling of affluence among households, MFI also accelerated the opening of new superstores and the modernization of some of its existing ones. The new design and format of the superstores were aimed at further transforming the image of MFI from a mainly cash-and-carry type of retailer to a company that also attracted the more affluent customers. These targeted customers had previously tended to visit the traditional High Street furniture retailer or department store. An essential feature of the superstore layout was that customers could see furniture in room settings from a single walkway that guided them through the store and encouraged them to view the whole range. The higher disposable incomes of many people, their willingness to use more credit, and the role of decor and furnishings in demonstrating social class made it very important that MFI continued to change its image. MFI eventually succeeded in widening its appeal to higher income groups without weakening its position in the market for lower priced products. Being able to appeal increasingly to a wider range of households was an important factor in the years of recession and rising unemployment that followed.

Expanding demand and the advantages of vertical integration

MFI had long recognized the importance of vertical integration. This form of expansion means that MFI no longer has to pay prices to major suppliers that include the latter's profit margins. The company can also ensure that, in the event of a sudden and large upturn in consumer spending, customers' orders are turned into deliveries that meet the agreed dates.

In order to maximize the potential benefits of vertical integration it was vital that MFI developed an efficient communication system between manufacturing and distribution activities. The application of developments in information technology gave sales staff access, via computer screens, to detailed information about product availability and delivery times while they were talking with customers. If the product was not in stock in the

	1985	1986	1987	1988	1989	1990	1991	1992	1993
Turnover(£m)	330.1	356.3	427.4	491.8	601.7	594.9	623.1	647.4	603.9
Operating profit (£m)	53.2	49.7	60.3	79.0	91.8	52.6	45.6	72.3	50.5
Average number of employees (full-time equivalents)	4,550	5,167	5,707	6,245	7,610	8,025	8,222	7,848	7,579
Sales per square foot (£)	86.51	85.66	86.78	95.08	110.03	97.33	95.98	100.23	96.12
Retail area at period end (000s square feet)	4,187	4,720	5,072	4,994	5,709	5,978	6,231	6,117	6,036
Capital expenditure (£m)	–	–	54.8	54.6	107.6	24.4	17.8	16.7	23.2
Stocks (£m)	–	–	60.7	61.4	106.5	72.8	71.5	69.6	65.3

MFI Furniture Group plc – financial performance.

superstore the salesperson could obtain a reliable date for delivery based upon the manufacturing and distribution schedule for the factory where the product was made. The computer system would then be used to raise specific orders for individual customers and this would help to ensure reliable delivery.

MFI had also recognized that, while speed of delivery was certainly significant for customers, what was more important in the case of major purchases such as bedrooms, kitchens and upholstery was keeping to the agreed date. This allowed customers to schedule delivery to fit in with any renovation, decoration or home improvement they were carrying out. In some situations, a delivery that was too early could be as inconvenient as a late delivery.

Vertical integration also meant that during these periods of strong demand the company did not experience the kinds of delays and shortages that are faced by those retailers who deal with independent manufacturers. These manufacturers may not have the capacity to cope with an increase in the size of orders from a larger number of retailers, and those retailers will lose market share because of shortages of stock and customer dissatisfaction with much longer delivery times. Because most of MFI's products are sourced internally its supplies were more secure and it was able to strengthen further its competitive position in terms of delivery dates. It was also able to ensure that higher sales were not achieved at the expense of a deterioration in the quality of its products.

This form of integration meant that production schedules for various products could be adjusted at short notice in response to changes in customer demand. During a period of rising demand the manufacturing operations are of great value to the competitive position of MFI's stores. Changes in the actual productive capacity in its factories and distribution system could also be brought about more quickly in response to changes in both the total demand and the demand for different types of products. MFI could also react more quickly to the kinds of design preferences expressed by people as these trends could be more rapidly transformed into new lines.

The return of unemployment and its effect upon MFI

The UK furniture market had grown in both value and volume as a result of the consumer spending boom of the late 1980s. This much improved market demand did not last very long, however, because the government became very concerned about the kinds of developments described in the diagram on page 11. There was a serious rise in the rate of inflation and this caused the government to take action that drastically reduced total spending. Between 1989 and 1991, therefore, there was only modest growth in the value of furniture sales but a clear decline in the actual volume of sales.

The government decision to depress total demand in the economy was also prompted by the dramatic decline in performance that the UK faced in relation to its international trade. This decline was due to the high rate of inflation, which made UK exports more expensive to foreigners while also making imported products relatively more attractive on the UK market. A large part of the increase in consumer spending tended to go on consumer durables such as cars, electrical goods and home entertainment products. Because overseas producers held strong positions in these markets this meant a further rapid rise in imports. The buoyant home demand helped to widen the

trade deficit further. It did this by causing a shortage in capacity among many UK firms, and rather than face long delivery dates more of their customers switched to overseas suppliers. The rise in spending also meant increased imports of materials, parts, components, machinery and equipment. A lack of capacity – and the lengthening delivery times that resulted – also meant that UK producers lost export orders.

The government responded to these developments by depressing consumer spending. To do this it relied almost exclusively upon raising interest rates. As described on page 12, this produced a sudden and large fall in consumer spending. The subsequent fall in output as companies cut back on production resulted in a rise in unemployment. The economy very soon entered a serious recession and this was aggravated after a while by other major economies also showing signs of falling industrial output.

The furniture market was bound to be hit by the fall in consumer spending and the rise in unemployment. Three main factors can be identified.

1   Even those in work cut back on their spending on consumer durables because as they saw other people losing their jobs in large numbers they feared that they might be next for redundancy. This fall in consumer confidence discouraged many households from spending large sums on consumer durables such as furniture. They preferred to save more of their income instead.

2   Consumers also reduced their take-up of new consumer credit because of the problems they would face in keeping up repayments if they were to lose their job.

3   Those households that had taken out mortgages at the height of the house price boom found themselves in a particularly tight financial position. They would have to make large cuts in other areas to meet the higher repayments and such households were also unlikely to take out any new consumer credit when other loans and hire-purchase debts had been cleared.

The overall effect of government economic policies upon consumer spending is shown in the following graphs.

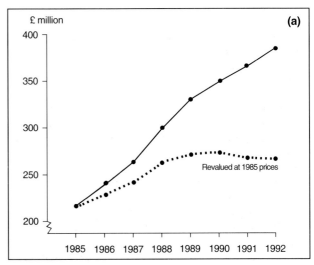

Total consumer expenditure 1985–92.

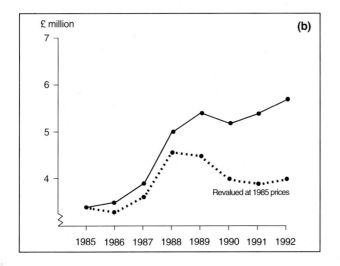

Expenditure on furniture and floor coverings 1985–92.

The slump in the housing market and its effect upon MFI

The rise in interest rates not only brought the period of booming house prices to an end but eventually produced a situation that very few people in the financial world ever thought would arise. This was an actual fall in the general level of house prices. The higher costs of mortgages, the lack of job opportunities in other areas, and fear of redundancy produced a large fall in the demand for houses. This obviously had a severe effect upon the demand for furniture, soft furnishings, floor coverings and DIY products.

The fall in house prices further depressed consumer confidence and hence consumer spending. Many households were suffering from what became known as 'negative equity'. In the previous period, people's willingness to take on large amounts of credit had been encouraged by the greater feeling of wealth generated by the rapid and seemingly endless rise in the price of their house. The unexpected fall in house prices, however, had left many people with a house worth less than they paid for it, or even, in some cases, less than their outstanding mortgage. This, together with the fear of unemployment, prompted them to cut down on non-essential spending such as the replacement of furnishings. For many people, even selling their house would not clear their mortgage, or any other debt, and this further depressed the level of consumer confidence.

Trading conditions started to deteriorate from about March 1989, and by 1990 the economy as a whole was in a deepening recession. During a period of depressed demand companies must be even more competitive if they are to ride out such an unfavourable business environment. If there are fewer customers in the market then the competition between suppliers will be all the more intense. In the case of MFI it also had to face the effect of higher interest charges on its existing borrowing, and in 1989 these were already running at some £60 million.

MFI responded to the anticipated decline in sales by tightening its control over costs and stocks in order both to offer attractive prices and to protect its profit margins. Savings were achieved in several ways:

1 A significant proportion of MFI's staff are employed on a temporary or part-time basis, and this allowed the company to slim down its workforce more in keeping with the lower sales.

2 MFI's flexible working practices also meant that employees took on a range of tasks and this meant that the company could shift and use them in ways that helped to save on labour costs.

3 The further application of computer systems also made MFI less labour-intensive both within the stores and in distribution. Together with a continuing restraint on pay rises this meant that labour costs fell to only 20 per cent of total costs.

4 By mid-1989 MFI had curtailed its capital spending plans for new stores and the twenty that did open in the two years after April 1989 were the result of commitment in the earlier period.

5 The company's policy of continually applying advances in information technology also helped to reduce costs. New computer systems meant that goods could be delivered to stores 'just in time' and this produced a major reduction in warehouse space and the costs of holding stocks. This has also meant that the optimum size for superstores in large towns has been reduced to 30,000 square feet of which about 30 per cent is warehouse space compared with about 40 per cent in the older stores. Further improvements in stock control and cost savings were achieved with the introduction of a new Electronic Point of Sale (EPOS) system and the benefits of these developments can be seen in the reduction in stocks shown in the table on page 15. The introduction of information technology and changes in systems meant that the whole business had become demand-led rather than production-led, and the manufacture of items and their flow through the supply chain were triggered by customer orders.

6 Because the company could operate with reduced stock levels, less warehouse space was needed both centrally and in the stores where improved designs also saved on floor space. Thus one-third of its distribution warehouse in Northampton is now sub-leased and earns a useful income while surplus space in the stores has been let to non-competing retailers.

MFI's National Distribution Centre.

7   MFI also introduced special self-service areas for the smaller, lower priced flat-pack items sold under the Pronto brand, and the range was extended in some stores to about 400 different lines compared with the usual 260. An increase in the sales of these products was another justification for the company's strategy of marketing a range of products to suit different income groups. In times of recession this range would be particularly attractive.

8   Although MFI has a substantial fleet of delivery vehicles to supply its stores, it also uses contractors during peak periods. During the period of depressed demand, the costs associated with spare capacity in its transport facilities were therefore not as serious as they would have been if it had owned more vehicles. Transport costs were also saved because some furniture items that were previously delivered direct from the factory to individual customers could now be stored for a short period in some of the space made available in the stores (see point 4 above).

9   MFI is an important customer for its suppliers. During a period of low demand in the economy, the suppliers would be even more concerned than usual with keeping their business with MFI and thus ensuring that they avoided price increases. This pressure upon suppliers was therefore another factor that helped MFI to control its own costs – and hence prices – and thus protect its financial position.

Towards the end of 1992 the government introduced the first of a series of cuts in interest rates. Inflation had by then fallen to a more acceptable level but now the real concern was the deep recession and high unemployment. It was hoped that lower rates of interest would stimulate consumer spending and encourage firms to increase their investment programmes. By the middle of 1993, however, there had been no significant and persistent upturn in the economy. Although there had occasionally been some signs of a recovery in levels of consumer confidence and spending, these had not generally lasted for long. Recovery in the housing market was both slow and patchy, and unemployment remained at a high level. Interest rates were in fact much lower than those that helped to trigger the spending and housing boom of the late 1990s. However, perhaps many households still clearly remembered the problems they faced when they took on more credit and larger mortgages only to see interest rates rise to very high levels.

ACTIVITIES

Short answer questions

1   Why did MFI give branding and market segmentation such an important part in its marketing strategy?
2   What developments have helped to increase the demand for home office furniture?
3   What factors will have exerted an upward pressure on MFI's unit costs during the late 1980s?
4   Why will a decision not to raise tax allowances and tax bands reduce the pressure of consumer spending in the economy?
5   List the kinds of products where demand is likely to be closely related to people moving home.
6   Increases in VAT and excise duties ease the pressures of demand in the economy because their overall effect is to reduce the average level of real income. Explain this statement.
7   Why will cuts in government spending on roads and defence eventually lead to a fall in the demand for furniture?
8   Give reasons why a fall in consumer spending is likely to cause firms to cut back on their capital projects.
9   Why will rising unemployment and falling consumer demand create an environment that reduces the rate of increase in unit labour costs?
10 Why has the application of information technology helped both to control MFI's costs and to strengthen its competitive position generally?

Case study

Assume that a young couple with a combined income of £18,000 and two children under 6 years old take out an interest-only mortgage for £60,000 in 1988 at the rate shown in the following table. The capital sum would be paid off at the end of the period by way of an endowment policy. The first £30,000 of the mortgage qualified for tax relief at the 25 per cent rate.

	Mortgage rate (%)
1982	13.00
1983	10.67
1984	11.38
1985	13.17
1986	11.84
1987	11.62
1988	10.86
1989	13.58
1990	15.05
1991	12.85
1992	10.25
1993*	8.01
*May	

1   After making an allowance for tax relief, what is the actual rate of interest paid on the first £30,000 of the mortgage?
2   Taking account of the changes in mortgage rates, calculate the monthly repayments in 1988, 1990 and May 1993.
3   How would you expect this couple to change their spending plans as a result of changes in mortgage interest payments?

Media analysis

Soon after the annual November Budget the newspapers report on the event by estimating how the changes in taxes and allowances will effect the spending power of different kinds of households according to their total income and pattern of spending.

1   *Investigate how these effects were reported after the last Budget. Alternatively, if the next Budget is in the near future, then prepare to collect the relevant newspaper articles when they are published the next day. Use the information to complete the following:*

(a) Make a list of the changes that the Chancellor of the Exchequer made to income tax rates, tax bands and allowances.

(b) Report on how these changes were likely to effect various income groups and how they might effect the sales of MFI's products.

2 Read the article below and then answer the questions that follow.

Inflation rate rises by more than forecast and manufacturing output declines

Recovery hopes dealt double blow

By Peter Norman and Emma Tucker

Hopes of sustained, non-inflationary recovery in Britain were dealt a double blow yesterday with news of a fall in manufacturing output over the summer and a higher-than-expected rise in retail prices last month.

Manufacturing output fell by a seasonally adjusted 0.4 per cent in August, confounding City expectations of a 0.4 per cent rise in the month, while the annual rate of retail price inflation quickened for the third successive month to 1.8 per cent in September, up sharply from June's 1.2 per cent low.

More worrying for Mr Kenneth Clarke, the chancellor, who meets his ministers and senior Treasury officials tomorrow to discuss his first Budget on November 30, was September's rise to 3.3 per cent in underlying inflation, excluding mortgage interest payments, from 3.0 per cent in the year to August.

Central Statistical Office figures also showed that growth in industrial production faltered during the summer with manufacturing output down 0.7 per cent in the three months to August 31 compared with the previous three-month period.

Yesterday's figures, following closely on Monday's news of a widening trade deficit and rising producer price inflation,

underlined the fragility of the UK recovery and pointed to a narrowing of Mr Clarke's room for manœuvre in the Budget.

Weak output might undermine any plans for a tax rise to cut Britain's £50 bn annual budget deficit.

The increase in underlying inflation to within the top quarter of the government's 1 to 4 per cent target range may limit his scope for a rise in indirect taxes such as value added tax and affect his ability to cut interest rates to offset fiscal tightening.

City analysts said the figures were disappointing, but the Treasury and the Bank of England said the recovery was still on track. The Bank said it expected inflation to remain in its target range and recalled that the rise in underlying inflation had been forecast in its August report.

Mr Stephen Dorrell, financial secretary to the Treasury, said Britain was still heading for a 3 per cent growth in mid-1994 and denied the recovery was dying. 'We never said this would proceed in a straight line,' Mr Dorrell said.

The increase in headline and underlying inflation reflected widespread price rises for retail goods, including dearer petrol and secondhand cars.

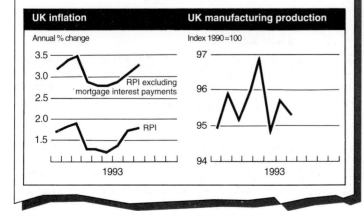

(a) Why did a 'weak output' make it difficult for the Chancellor to raise taxes to reduce the level of government borrowing?

(b) What might a rise in VAT have added to inflationary pressures?

(c) Why might the rise in inflation create a problem for the Chancellor if he cut interest rates to help offset the depressing effects of any tax increases he introduced?

(d) What developments described in the article are likely to effect the demand for MFI's products?

Data analysis

The data in the following table show how the value of the pound fluctuated against certain currencies from 1980 until mid-1993.

	1985	1990	1991	1992	1993	1994
France						
Franc	10.84	9.82	9.70	8.37	8.74	8.46
Germany						
Deutsche Mark	3.54	2.89	2.84	2.45	2.57	2.48
Italy						
Lira	2414.80	2177.00	2148.75	2231.00	2533.00	2388.04
Netherlands						
Guilder	3.99	3.26	3.20	2.76	2.87	2.79
Spain						
Peseta	221.25	183.70	180.65	173.80	211.46	202.08
Norway						
Krone	10.97	11.35	11.16	10.47	11.13	10.78
Finland						
Markka	7.79	7.00	7.73	7.94	8.57	8.11
Canada						
Dollar	2.02	2.24	2.16	1.93	1.96	2.05
USA						
Dollar	1.45	1.93	1.87	1.51	1.48	1.48

*All figures end December, except 1994 which are end March

Sterling exchange rates (Currency Units per pound)
Source: Barclays Bank: International Financial Statistics, IMF.

1 Assume that a given quantity of a particular type of timber imported by MFI from Norway in 1985 was priced at 548.5 Krone.

(a) Calculate the changes in cost in sterling of importing this raw material to MFI between 1985 and 1990 and then between 1990 and March 1994.

(b) Repeat the calculations for the same timber imported from Sweden at 548 Krona, Finland at 389.5 Markka, Canada at 101 Dollars and the USA at 72.5 Dollars.

(c) During those periods when the exchange rate falls, what can MFI do to absorb the effects of higher raw material prices and avoid price rises?

(d) How can MFI use a rise in the exchange rate to improve its competitive position?

2 Assume that in 1990 MFI manufactured a particular kitchen design which sold in its French outlets for 11,640 Francs. What would have been the cost to French customers in March 1994 on the basis of sterling having risen by 5 per cent during that period?

The role of an information system
British Airways
3

Introduction

British Airways is the world's leading international airline. In 1992 it was the sixth largest in the world when measured in terms of the total load (passengers and cargo) carried on scheduled flights multiplied by the distance they are flown. This measurement is used by the airline industry to assess the relative size of operators, and in 1993 British Airways' scheduled services produced 16,695 million tonne kilometres (i.e. load in tonnes × kilometres flown). British Airways' pre-tax profit in the financial year 1992–3 also made it the third most profitable airline in the world. The major reasons for this are considered by the company to be cost control and high quality service.

In 1992–3, the British Airways Group carried 28 million passengers, of which nearly 26 million were on scheduled services. That is the equivalent of more than fifty passengers checking in every minute. In 1992 more than 20 million passengers travelled on its international route network – 5 million more than its nearest competitor. British Airways was also the world's sixth largest international cargo airline, and in 1992–3 it carried more than 500,000 tonnes of freight and mail. In the summer of 1993 the airline offered scheduled flights to 155 destinations in seventy-two countries. Its route network covered more than 600,000 kilometres, which is equivalent to over forty times around the world.

British Airways' main base is at Heathrow, the largest international airport in the world, where it competes with about ninety other airlines. At Gatwick it faces competition from some ninety-five airlines, and in the UK market alone there are about 200 other carriers with which it has to compete. The British Airways Group, along with its affiliated companies in Europe, Deutsche BA (Germany) and TAT European Airlines (France), has the largest fleet in Western Europe. In 1993 British Airways had over 240 aircraft and in March of that year it had a further sixty-eight aircraft on order with the possibility of another sixty-three. It is the world's second largest operator of Boeing 747s and one of only two airlines operating Concorde, the world's only supersonic passenger aircraft. In 1992–3 British Airways' aircraft operated 268,000 flights, which is equivalent to one British Airways flight taking off or landing every two minutes, 24 hours a day, every day of the year. British Airways also has investments in USAir and Qantas. This has allowed the company to obtain an interest in the major markets of North America and the Pacific

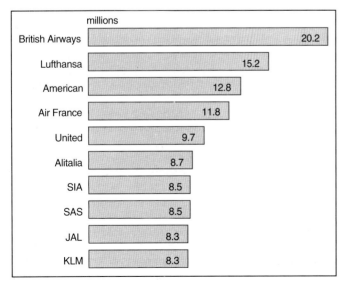

International scheduled passengers 1992.

	millions	
British Airways		20.2
Lufthansa		15.2
American		12.8
Air France		11.8
United		9.7
Alitalia		8.7
SIA		8.5
SAS		8.5
JAL		8.3
KLM		8.3

OUR MISSION

To be the best and most successful company in the airline industry.

OUR GOALS

Safe and Secure
To be a safe and secure airline.

Financially Strong
To deliver a strong and consistent financial performance.

Global Leader
To secure a leading share of air travel business worldwide with a significant presence in all major geographical markets.

Service and Value
To provide overall superior service and good value for money in every market segment in which we compete.

Customer Driven
To excel in anticipating and quickly responding to customer needs and competitor activity.

Good Employer
To sustain a working environment that attracts, retains and develops committed employees who share in the success of the company.

Good Neighbour
To be a good neighbour, concerned for the community and the environment.

British Airways' Mission and goals.

region. British Airways is a significant operator of package tours and the Group has its own charter airline, Caledonian Airways. It also sells its services to other companies in such areas as aircraft and passenger handling, engineering, training and information technology.

Because British Airways is such a huge worldwide operation it must provide a high quality customer service. This in turn means that it must have efficient systems for communicating information to all those employees responsible for meeting the needs of its customers. Its management information system must also ensure that the airline operates and achieves its goals in a cost-efficient manner.

The general role of a management information system

Information is a vital resource for organizations that have to exist in a competitive market. Efficient production, marketing, distribution and cost control depend upon the availability of timely and reliable information. Managers require information about the performance of the organization as a whole, its component parts and perhaps also individual employees in key positions. All organizations therefore need a management information system.

Management needs information in order to monitor the various aspects of its operations, support its decision-making, control the organization and plan its future. The system itself is the means by which various kinds of business data are processed and converted into the kinds of information required by employees in different departments. Much of the information received by a particular department or section may be subject to further processing and then passed on to others in a different format from that in which it was originally received.

For example, data can be processed in order to establish the amount of business done by each of the 100 shops and sales offices that are operated by British Airways in the UK and around the world. This kind of information will be important for many aspects of the company's operations such as:

- total sales;
- selling costs;
- analysing the effects of advertising or promotions;
- the expansion of sales outlets;
- the further development of telesales centres;
- productivity, staffing and training;
- the further application of information technology to the reservation systems.

Information that relates to one aspect of an organization's operations may also act as the raw data needed by other sections. These sections will then combine it with data received from other sources to obtain additional information connected with its business.

Where information is needed

Information must be processed so that it meets the needs of the various levels of an organization's activities. It is required at three main levels: operational, middle management and senior management.

Operational level

At the operational level, whether on the workshop floor or in the office, there will be supervisors responsible for ensuring that certain aspects of the 'productive' work are planned and carried out efficiently. In the case of British Airways, its main goal is for its aircraft to be safe and secure. The aircraft go through a maintenance cycle that ranges from checks carried out on a daily basis and those undertaken just before a flight to major services every 24,000 flying hours (or every five years if this is sooner). These major services involve 180 engineers over periods of between 20 and 25 days. The engineers at British Airways responsible for organizing and supervising each stage of the maintenance and overhaul of aircraft will need the following kinds of information in relation to the inspection, testing and repair of the various systems and parts:

- reports from the flight crew and cabin staff on minor problems;
- reports on earlier work carried out on the aircraft;
- manuals, drawings and maintenance schedules;
- materials, components and equipment required;
- availability of plant and machine capacity;
- the availability of the necessary electrical and mechanical engineering skills to carry out various operations;
- start and completion dates.

At the operational level, much information is also required about the flight itself. The flight crew needs information from the Operations Department, which monitors closely the comings and goings of British Airways aircraft worldwide, and coordinates the activities at British Airways stations in different parts of the world. The flight crew will plan the flight themselves within the limits set down by air traffic controllers. If particular atmospheric conditions such as strong tail winds are likely to affect the flight, then Operations will be aware of this and offer the captain of the flight various routeing options. The cabin crew will also be given information about the flight ahead. They need to know the number of passengers and whether there are unaccompanied children, passengers in wheelchairs or others who may need particular assistance or special dietary requirements. In this way they can give an individual service to each passenger.

Many of the passengers will have booked directly by contacting one of the telephone salespeople at British Airways' telesales centres. These sales teams need immediate access to a mass of information, such as details of British Airways' scheduled route network, seat availability and fare structures. They will also need information that allows them to arrange hotels and car hire services.

In any organization, certain kinds of information are essential for those who plan, control and take decisions at the operational level, where the production of the goods or provision of the services actually takes place. The work carried out at this level of the organization will then give rise to data that will be processed to provide much of the information required at management level.

Middle management level

The information required by middle management personnel will be largely concerned with the efficiency with which operations are carried out and the extent to which the resources under their control are being used to achieve the organization's objectives. Much of this information will therefore be concerned with the productivity of labour and machinery and with the rate at which materials and other inputs are used up. This data is used to monitor and take decisions relating to the control of those factors that affect costs, revenues, profits and the achievement of the organization's objectives. Middle management will therefore require a great deal of information of a financial nature, and in the case of British Airways this will revolve around such areas as:

- revenue from passengers, freight, mail and services sold to other companies;
- employee costs;
- depreciation;
- the costs of leased aircraft;
- fuel and oil costs;
- engineering and other aircraft costs;
- landing fees and *en route* charges;
- handling charges, catering and other operating costs;
- selling costs.

The latest wide-bodied jet aircraft cost tens of millions of pounds; it is essential therefore that British Airways ensures that they are utilized as fully as possible. This will involve information relating to such matters as:

- the average number of hours of aircraft utilization per aircraft per year;
- load factors to establish the percentage of available seats and cargo-carrying capacity that were actually sold;
- total revenue from the sale of passenger tickets;
- the number of passenger kilometres (i.e. the number of passengers carried × the distance flown);
- the amount of passenger revenue earned per passenger kilometre;
- total revenue from the carrying of cargo;
- the number of cargo tonne kilometres (i.e. the number of tonnes of cargo carried × the distance flown);
- cargo revenue per cargo tonne kilometre.

Senior management level

At the level of senior management, important information will be derived from both internal and external sources. Planning and decision-making about the organization's objectives and strategies will require information about broad areas of its business rather than the more specific and perhaps detailed information needed for decision-making at the lower levels. Senior management will therefore require information concerning such matters as:

- overall profitability and the contribution that each part of its business makes to total profit;
- capital requirements and the position in relation to internally generated capital and the availability and cost of external sources of capital;
- personnel requirements;
- forecasts concerning the future levels of demand in the markets where its products/services are sold.

The need to support internally generated data with that from external sources will be particularly important, for example, in the case of assessing current and future competitiveness and future market prospects. Information will be required about such areas as:

- developments in internal costs and recent trends in own sales;
- changes in the markets where the organization obtains its labour, capital, materials and other inputs;
- the strategies currently being followed by competitors;
- the likely effects upon its operations and markets of economic, social, political and legal changes.

The kinds of issues that would concern senior management at British Airways would include:

- regional conflicts that would affect air travel to particular areas;
- the growth in incomes in different countries, the level of world trade and those countries experiencing the most rapid rate of economic growth (in 1992, for example, the International Air Traffic Association forecast that air travel would grow by about 6 per cent a year until the year 2000 and that the most rapid rate of growth would be in the North East Asian markets);
- the opportunities offered by further deregulation whereby governments around the world agree to the removal of restrictions that seek to protect the interests of their own airlines;
- the effects of greater competition on fares;
- the introduction of new routes;
- the development of new aircraft and their possible lease/purchase;
- mergers/takeovers/partnerships that would increase market opportunities;
- cost reduction programmes such as the one introduced in 1991 known as 'gap closure', which was aimed at dealing with the downturn in business and profits produced by the Gulf War and which during its first two years produced savings of over £400 million;
- negotiations with trade unions concerning changes in working practices aimed at raising productivity and saving on labour costs;
- training and motivational schemes such as the 'Winning For Customers' programme introduced in 1992;
- additional capital projects such as those concerned with improving comfort and widening the facilities for British Airways' customers such as new lounges at both Heathrow and Gatwick;
- researching the needs of the different segments of the market to develop further the level of service provided to customers under British Airways' main 'brands', such as Concorde, First, Club World, Club Europe and World Traveller;

All three levels of an organization need information that will allow them to make the best use of the resources under their control to achieve their particular objectives as efficiently as possible. This is as true of senior management taking decisions about the allocation of capital funds between alternative projects as it is of supervisors deciding how to deploy the labour and machinery between the various operations or processes for which they are responsible. Having taken such decisions, they will then need information on what progress is being made and how efficiently the project or work is being carried out. Whatever the nature and purpose of information it must be communicated in the most effective way.

Communication methods and channels

The channel used to communicate information will depend upon a combination of the following factors:

- the need for an immediate feedback or response;
- cost;
- speed and urgency;
- accuracy;
- the number and location of the people who need the information;
- confidentiality;
- the desired degree of formality/informality;
- convenience;
- complexity and amount of detail;
- the type of information, e.g. financial, statistical, plans, drawings, rules and regulations, job description;
- the need to keep a record of the information supplied.

The media used for communicating the information can be selected from the following:

- written reports;
- manuals containing the instructions connected with certain procedures, operations or methods of production;
- letters with necessary enclosures;
- circulars and memorandums;
- notice-boards;
- the organization's own magazine or newspaper;
- sheets of figures or standard forms containing numerical or other types of information under specific headings;
- graphs, charts, drawings, photographs, video-tapes, closed-circuit television, films and other visual techniques;
- meetings and interviews;
- telephone calls;
- fax communications;
- public address announcements;
- electronic mail and network messaging.

The process of developing new information technology services itself involves using existing IT systems.

Computer systems are important not only for communication but for processing and producing much information communicated through many of the other channels.

Whatever the method used, the information itself should be relevant to the needs of the recipient and should avoid superfluous comments and unnecessary detail. The information communicated to a supervisor in a factory may have to include an exact description of the operations to be carried out and their numerical values. This would contrast with the much broader information supplied to middle and senior management. The latter may require only general indicators and a broad description of the internal and external developments that need to be considered when assessing the organization's performance, setting objectives and deciding upon strategies.

Exception reporting

To ensure that the information provided to management is relevant, clear and concise and makes effective use of managers' time, it may be restricted to data relating to 'exceptional' developments. Middle management, for example, may only need information connected with those measurements of performance that deviate by more than a certain percentage from the targets established for them. The information dealing with an exceptional performance in relation to a particular measurement should also be supported by concise statements of the internal and/or external factors that may have contributed to such developments. For example, a vital aspect of the quality of British Airways' service is keeping to its departure and arrival times. Flight schedules, however, can be affected by adverse weather, the demands of air traffic control, or industrial action by external organizations. Management will need to be informed, along with reasons, if the proportion of flights that fail to keep within 15 minutes of scheduled times is greater than, say, 80 per cent over a certain period of time. Exception reporting can make a more effective use of the time and skills of middle managers.

Vertical information flow

This refers to the direction of the communication channel. A downward information flow describes the provision of information by a superior to an immediate subordinate and can cover the following areas:

1 the issuing of instructions, which involves the delegating of work and information concerning the objective and targets to be achieved by the subordinate;
2 procedures, working methods and practices and the rules and regulations that have been established by the organization;
3 information about how the subordinate's job and performance will contribute to the efficient conduct of other aspects of the organization's activities and hence the overall objectives of the organization;
4 an actual assessment of the subordinate's performance.

Some information will not come from a worker's immediate superior; general information dealing with the structure and goals of the organization and the kind of information provided by the personnel department when the employee first starts work come from other areas. In the case of information that relates to the work undertaken by the subordinate, however, the communication channel will be from superior to immediate subordinate.

An upward information flow is from a subordinate to a superior. This may be the feedback from a downward flow or it may originate from the subordinates themselves. An upward flow can deal with the following areas:

- the provision of information required by a superior;
- information about the subordinate's own performance, problems and aspirations;
- information about other employees in the subordinate's section and relations with sections with which there is a direct link;
- ideas on improved working methods and practices and possible solutions to any problems that have been identified.

Horizontal information flow

This describes the passing of information between people of the same status. Because many of the operations within an organization are interdependent, formal arrangements must exist for the exchange of information to promote the highest degree of cooperation between sections and departments. In the case of the production department, for example, there will have to be close contact with the purchasing department on such matters as changes to materials and components and the potential use of more advanced and efficient machinery and equipment. Similarly there will have to be close contact between the various activities that contribute to marketing, such as advertising, market research, and transport and distribution.

Frequency

Some information, such as that relating to industrial or manufacturing operations, may be required many times during the course of a single working day to ensure that the work is carried out smoothly and efficiently. Much of the information required by middle management however may be prepared on a weekly or monthly basis. This is often the case with accounting information that is used for measuring performance and for control purposes. Senior management may also need information that reports on both internal and external developments arising over a longer period. More frequent information relating to much shorter periods of time is unlikely to depict trends or problems and would be a waste of the resources devoted to its collection and analysis.

Another important aspect of the collection of information is timing. Information should be timed to meet the different needs of the various levels of management and control. Operational information required by supervisors must be updated and communicated on a very regular basis. Middle management will not be able to function efficiently if the information reported to it is either premature or too late to be used for the purposes of management control. This is because the decisions made on the basis of the information may prove to be inappropriate in the light of more recent developments.

The quality of information

The essential characteristics of good information and an efficient information system can be summarized as follows.

1 The right people must receive the right information at the right time.
2 The information should be accurate and concise yet comprehensive enough to avoid a time-consuming request for extra information.

3 The information must be presented and communicated without ambiguity or possible misunderstanding.
4 The recipient of the information must have confidence in the ability of the sender and hence in the contents of the communication.
5 The sender must have confidence in the ability of the recipient to understand, use and take effective decisions based upon the information supplied.
6 The information must be relevant and hence of value. It must assist the recipient in taking decisions that make the most effective use of the organization's resources. It might also help in decisions concerning the possible introduction of new and improved working practices that raise productivity or other action that produces an improvement in profitability by reducing costs or increasing sales revenue.
7 The information system, the communication media and the kind of information provided should be periodically reviewed and adjusted to take into account any actual and potential developments within the organization itself and in response to external trends and changes. This is particularly necessary in connection with further advances in information technology.
8 Vertical and horizontal flows should be clearly defined. Confusion, combined perhaps with a lack of confidence in either the sender or recipient, may lead to the *ad hoc* growth of informal and uncoordinated information systems. These can result in alternative sources of information and a situation in which the different levels of management may receive inconsistent, inaccurate or even conflicting information.

To fly an aircraft at 35,000 feet, at a speed of 550 miles per hour, air crew must have a high level of confidence in the ground staff, and vice versa. Information must be always be completely accurate.

Computers and information management

Computers provide the means to store, summarize, analyse and present all kinds of information in a way that best suits the needs of managers and the problems they deal with. They can help organizations in a number of ways:

Quick reaction to changes in the business environment

The organization that can react quickly to changes in the business environment will strengthen its competitive position.

Reaction time is reduced by cutting down time lost through slow communications, lost messages and time-consuming searches through traditional filing systems. Computers replace the manual production and analysis of complex data or documents that may also require both the numerical and graphical presentation of statistical information.

Very few British Airways employees, whether senior managers, pilots, secretaries or chefs in catering bases, will go through their working day without accessing its computer network, directly or indirectly.

Processing complex information

Computers can be used to process information that helps to identify market opportunities and forecast potential problems in the business environment. Early provision of this information along with reduced reaction times will mean that opportunities can be exploited and action taken to minimize problems.

Administrative support

Higher productivity is also achieved by using such techniques as electronic mail and word processing.

Increasing job satisfaction

Computer technology can increase job satisfaction by reducing the amount of time spent by individuals in repetitive and routine processes. The range of responsibilities undertaken by an individual employee and the scope of their decision-making could often be restricted by the amount and range of information that they had access to or were able to handle. Computer technology, however, allows employees to have much broader and therefore more interesting jobs because all the data they require can be provided at their fingertips. This can contribute to greater job satisfaction, and the overall improvement in morale can be reflected in a rise in productivity.

Collecting information at source

Computers allow information to be collected close to the source of the operation or transaction. For example, a great variety of information can be obtained by processing the data recorded and stored by the electronic cash registers used at a supermarket's check-outs. This will be communicated not only to the supermarket manager but also directly to the warehouse that supplies the supermarket and to the organization's head office. Portable terminals and personal computers now mean that salespeople, engineers and construction workers can refer to a central office data base, enter transactions and receive work schedules or sales leads at the place where they happen to be

operating at the time. As new, more transportable hardware is developed, employees can work at home or while travelling on a train or aeroplane.

Accessing information outside the company

Terminals can be put into the hands of customers or other organizations likely to be a source of business. Airlines, for example, have terminals in travel agents in order to attract reservations. Distribution and manufacturing organizations can install terminals on the premises of their major customers.

Reducing errors

Unless the operator inputs incorrect data or overrides and intervenes in the system, the level and frequency of mistakes should be reduced significantly or even eliminated.

British Airways and information management

The world's airlines used to take their bookings over the telephone, or by telex, and a team of clerks would manually enter the current seats on each flight on large boards lined up on the wall. This system was suitable some sixty years ago when there were many fewer flights and aircraft had only thirty-five seats, but the size of British Airways' operations described on page 20 requires an information management system based upon the latest computer technology. The Information Management Department at British Airways is thus larger than many specialist computer companies and the use of information technology is vital to its success. This department's mission is 'to achieve business advantage for British Airways through being the world leader in the application of airline Information Technology'.

Scope of activity

Information Management (IM) is the department that looks after all British Airways' ground telecommunications, radio and computing systems worldwide. It employs staff specially to design and support systems that help the airline keep ahead of its competitors. In 1992, IM invested over £49 million in hardware, including computer terminals, radios, and computer mainframes and over £12 million in software such as Reservations, and Engineering systems. The department has:

- nearly 2,000 staff worldwide;
- two main data centres at Heathrow, housing fourteen mainframe computer complexes;
- over 160 mid-range processors;
- over 14,000 personal computers;
- 44,000 computer devices in over 750 locations worldwide;
- 200,000 connected terminals worldwide.

IM also sells software, data services, training and consultancy. In 1992 it sold to 140 airlines and commercial companies and earned £23 million. The forecast sales target for 1993 was £27 million.

British Airways Systems

British Airways uses over 300 systems. These range from the provision of the kind of information needed to manage its fleet of aircraft down to the tracking of cargo and baggage loading.

Airline Information Management System (AIMS)

AIMS is designed for senior management, and gives on-line access to a broad range of information about the airline and the industry. It provides an overview of British Airways' performance, including numbers of bookings, market share and information about competitors. It also gives general airline news, such as the number of Club passengers who flew the London–Paris route last week or recent movements in British Airways' shares compared with the rest of the stock market.

British Airways Business Systems (BABS)

BABS is a vital system for British Airways that operates continuously, 365 days a year. The heart of BABS is the passenger reservation system, which holds a record of every forward booking for passengers on British Airways and many other airlines. All the information about each passenger's booking is held in a Passenger Name Record (PNR). This records the flights, the number of seats required, the names and contact addresses, the ticket details and any special requirements or additional services such as hotel or car hire. At any one time, BABS holds over 2 million PNRs and about 100,000 of them change every day as a result of messages received at the rate of up to 200 per second all over the world.

Part of the process of booking an air journey is paying for it. BABS has a comprehensive fare quotation system with some 40,000,000 individual fares.

The Departure Control system is also run by BABS and the most visible part of this is the check-in system which records the passengers' arrival at the airport, cross-checks their reservations and allocates seats.

BABS also holds inventory records for each flight for each day of operation as it records the number of seats available for sale at a particular fare and the number of seats sold so far. Every time a booking is made or amended, the inventory is updated in order to keep track of what is available and when a flight is full.

BABS communicates with British Airways' sales offices and with many other reservations systems worldwide in order to take bookings. It also communicates with other British Airways computer systems to forward data for accounting, marketing analysis and flight operations. The system runs on four linked IBM mainframe computers, each capable of performing 22 million instructions per second.

Airline Ticket and Boarding passes (ATBs)

ATBs are progressively replacing Traditional Airline Tickets (TATs). The appeal of an ATB is that it combines, in one document, the passenger's receipt, ticket to travel, and boarding pass for clearance on to the aircraft. ATBs have the passenger and travel date details encoded in a magnetic stripe to an industry standard. This is on the reverse of the ATB and means that passengers carry with them, in machine-readable form, their travel details and information about the fare they have paid. The transition from TAT to ATB has been under way for some five years and will take many more years to complete. British Airways (along with Swissair, Scandinavian Airline Services and some of the big American carriers) has been one of the pioneers of ATB technology. Around the British Airways network, ATBs are installed at Heathrow, Birmingham, Paris, Chicago and Toronto.

Departure Control System (DCS)

The primary function of this system may be broken down into two main areas: (1) check-in and (2) weight and balance.

DCS eases the check-in process for both passengers and staff. The check-in process includes such factors as allocating seats to passengers while satisfying as far as possible their requirements for smoking or non-smoking and aisle or window seats. It stores details of all passengers travelling on a flight, including such information as name, destination, special meal requests, number of bags, etc. DCS issues passengers with boarding passes, thus allowing them access to the aircraft itself and indicating to them their seat numbers. Bag tags are also issued to ensure that all bags are loaded on to the correct flights and to provide a means of matching passengers with their bags.

The weight and balance function involves distributing the load on an aircraft in such a way that the plane is well balanced for the flight. Failure to do this may result in the plane being nose- or tail-heavy, which can adversely affect the performance of the aircraft. The DCS weight and balance system is designed to load the aircraft as close as possible to the ideal in order to achieve a smoother flight and economic rate of fuel consumption.

In both fields DCS is continually being expanded and upgraded, to provide better customer service for check-in, for example, or by amending the weight and balance system for new aircraft types such as Boeing 747–400.

Flight Information and Control of Operations (FICO)

The FICO system was initially developed in 1968. It is a computer system that receives data such as the schedule from a planning computer and allows the user to enquire about any information held or to amend it. It controls the day-to-day running of the airline. It also collects data from other systems, such as meteorological information from Bracknell, landing touchdown zones and finals from BASIS (British Airports Staff Information System) and departures and arrivals from FIND (Flight Information Display). It holds data on aircraft locations and is able to forecast times of arrivals, departures and delays. It passes information to other computer systems: for example, aircraft hours to aircraft records; statistics to IMS (Information Management System); arrival times to FIND; and schedules to other systems and ITV's ORACLE. FICO sends data updates all over the world. Some signals are sent automatically as soon as data is amended.

Flight Information Display (FIND)

FIND is used to run the minute-by-minute operations of the airline, which means that the information displayed is always up to date. It holds the 1,600 or so flights that make up today's and tomorrow's operations.

The FIND screen shows all the information that British Airways staff need in order to service and turn round a flight, such as arrival and departure time, any delay anticipated, destination, and where the aircraft is situated. It also displays information on cargo and mailbags and helps Operations supervisors decide how many people are required to load, clean, board and dispatch an aircraft.

FIND is continually updated, up to six times per minute at peak times. It receives information from FICO and all changes flash for one minute after they are made.

System for Worldwide Operational and Route Data (SWORD)

This system is used for the calculation of operational flight plans for all British Airways services. It holds a store of 'way points', which are the specific points over which an aircraft must fly on a given route.

The way points are strung together by the computer in the most effective way to take into account fuel levels, minimum flying time and weather. Before taking a flight, the flight crew will collect the SWORD plan for their route and this can be likened to a road map across the sky. It will give them direction, height, temperature, headwinds or tailwinds and fuel requirements, including extra fuel should they have to divert or contingency fuel in case they are unable to land immediately.

Total Inventory Management for Engineering (TIME)

TIME is a computerized inventory system that was launched in May 1987. It is designed to meet the needs of British Airways' engineering operations. The department's work covers such areas as the overhaul, repair and maintenance of 241 aircraft, the engines that power them and the vast number of sophisticated systems built into them. The functions of TIME include stock control, component tracking, requisitioning and shortage control. TIME thus ensures that the vital work of engineers is not delayed because parts and components are not readily available at the right time and place.

TIME has taken more than 100 worker-years to develop, plan and implement. It controls an inventory of nearly 500,000 Part Numbers. The engineers using the system generate around 2 million transactions per week using around 2,000 computer terminals and printers.

Computerized information systems play a major role in ensuring that British Airways' engineers can help deliver the safest possible service and one that flies on time.

Airline Inflight Product Management Planning Control (AIMPAC)

AIMPAC produces a catering order for each flight on a dedicated terminal at the contractor's premises and covers such areas as meals and drinks. The system links to BABS (see page 26) to work out a profile of booked passengers and thus to meet the catering requirements of particular flights. This enables excess catering to be minimized, improves British Airways' ability to check contractors' charges and streamlines the production and maintenance of documentation.

Kate

This system provides a central control for catering equipment and supplies to catering stations. It effectively forms the catering section's own stock control system, running 24 hours per day on one of British Airways' fourteen mainframes. It is used to ensure that any equipment, duty-free goods or dry goods that are required on any flight from any station are available when and where needed.

Computerized systems help to ensure a high-quality catering service on British Airways flights.

Barplus

Barplus is a wholly computerized in-flight sales and stock management system. It was developed by British Airways in response to the increasing importance, range and complexity of the in-flight sales operation. Barplus was designed to make the entire in-flight sales of duty-free items run more smoothly. The system is programmed with details of which duty-free goods have been taken from the bonded warehouse where they are stored and which are to be loaded aboard a particular flight. This replaces the usual time-consuming manual process. On board the aircraft, the compact Barplus unit sits neatly on the bar trolley to simplify sales transactions and customs declarations. It is also capable of analysing bar sales from previous flights and using the information to recommend a bar tailored to suit a specific route. Barplus eliminates the necessity for crew to complete by hand any paperwork related to in-flight sales. In addition, the 'card swipe' built into the Barplus unit reads credit cards electronically so that crew no longer need to fill in sales vouchers. It can also be programmed to take account of fluctuations in exchange rates, which means that prices will reflect such movements and change can be calculated in various currencies.

British Airways Recommended Stand Allocation Control (BARSAC)

BARSAC is a system in use by British Airways at Gatwick. The system reads a schedule of flight operations and, taking into account the size of the aircraft, the number of passengers on board and what the next flight is for that aircraft, makes a recommended stand allocation to the staff of Terminal Control. The stand is the position where a particular aircraft will eventually come to rest. Once this is confirmed, BARSAC shoots the selected stand into the system that broadcasts flight, time and location details to all operational sections of the airfield.

Bagtrac/Bahamas

Bagtrac and Bahamas are two related systems provided by SITA, an international organization concerned with aircraft communications. Both are involved in the reporting and tracing of bags that get separated from their owners during an air journey.

Bagtrac is used for reporting details of a lost bag (or a found bag without apparent owner). By matching lost and found bag reports from anywhere in the world, the system speeds up the reconciliation of bags with their owners.

Bahamas is the Airline Management Information System that provides members of SITA with summary details about quantities of lost baggage and the speed with which they are reconciled with their owners.

Networks

As a company operating in every continent of the world, British Airways needs strong communication links. These are provided by communication networks that speed the flow of information between computer centres, telephone sales offices, airports and all other operational areas. This information may be transmitted as voice or data or, in a growing number of instances, in a visual format. British Airways has a number of networks in operation to connect terminals to large computer installations and provide telephones to staff.

The data communications network means that British Airways' 33,000 computer terminals, located in over 200 sites all over the world, are able to tap into key corporate information stored in a complex of large mainframe computers.

The network is provided by a number of different technologies such as satellite links, undersea fibre-optic cables, and even high speed 'ring' networks that circle the main buildings at Heathrow Airport. Because it is such a vital resource, British Airways maintains a 24-hour Network Control Centre (NCC) to watch over the network to ensure the service is kept available at all times to all users.

In addition to data networks, British Airways staff provide a strong demand for networks that offer voice communication. Within the Heathrow airport region a telephone network with over 10,000 extensions is available for staff to go about their business. All the key telephone sales centres are connected by special systems to the public British Telecom and Mercury telephone networks to ensure speedy connection of public callers to sales agents.

Voice communication is also available by radio, primarily for communication between the aircraft and the operations centre, but also for mobile communications for staff in the terminals. In situations where voice is not enough, the latest trend is for video teleconferencing links where staff in different geographical areas can hold a face-to-face meeting without leaving base.

British Airways staff always have access to the most appropriate form of communication.

Activities
Short answer questions

1   What kinds of information from internal and external sources will be important to the management of British Airways when considering an expansion of its fleet of aircraft?

2   Give examples of the kind of information within British Airways that has to be continually updated.

3   Explain why various departments within British Airways will need data about the number of seat reservations made on different flights.

4   Explain the importance of the horizontal information flows between those in British Airways' engineering operations and the department responsible for supplies of parts, components and equipment.

5   What kinds of problems can arise if employees ignore clearly agreed channels and communicate informally with each other? What are the particular problems if this involves an employee dealing with someone who is in a position above that of their own superior?

6   Why might certain kinds of communications benefit from video links?

7   Describe the advantages to travel agents and airlines of advances in information technology when arranging flights for their clients.

8   In 1993 British Airways spent £560 million on fuel and oils. This was over 10 per cent of its total operating expenditure. Explain how British Airways' computerized management information systems help to minimize such fuel and oil costs.

9   Describe the different kinds of information received and processed by the various sections of an organization's financial department.

10 Explain why certain kinds of jobs benefit from employees having personal or portable computers that give them access to a central office data base when operating away from their own base.

Local Investigation

Tasks

1   Each student should select someone they know who works for a local company where they have certain operational, administrative or management responsibilities. Arrange a meeting with such a contact in order to obtain information in relation to the following:
    (a) the kinds of information they receive during the normal course of their job;
    (b) from whom it is received;
    (c) how it is communicated to them;
    (d) how frequently certain kinds of information are received;
    (e) the kind of information that they in turn then communicate to others in the organization and the positions that they hold;
    (f) how frequently the information in (e) is communicated and in what format;
    (g) the extent to which they are involved in retrieving information from or putting information into a computer system.
    Each student should then produce a brief written report on how a particular job involves receiving, processing and passing on certain kinds of information.
2   Refer to the media for communicating information listed on page 23 and in each case say under what circumstances they might be most appropriate for certain kinds of information.
3   Conduct a survey to identify the different kinds of communications media used in your school/college and the purposes for which they are used.
4   Use your school/college to construct a chart that outlines both its vertical and horizontal information flows and the positions held by both the relevant senders and receivers of the information.

Case study

Tasks

1   Explain why the senior management at British Airways is likely to be interested in data relating to the following kinds of developments:
    (a) a 15 per cent fall in the value of the pound against the US dollar and an average fall of 10 per cent fall in its value against major European currencies;
    (b) more rapid rates of economic growth in the economies of the Far East such as Malaysia, Thailand, South Korea and China;
    (c) a fall in the general level of interest rates in both the UK and other members of the European Union;
    (d) forecasts concerning the number of people who express a preference for using the Channel Tunnel and high speed rail links for reaching some of the major European cities;
    (e) a further rise in the average number of days holiday taken in the course of the working year;
2   Assume that you intend to travel abroad using one of British Airways' flights. Outline all the various aspects of your trip where the company's computerized management information systems will help to ensure that you receive the best possible service from the time you make your reservation to the time you are booked into your hotel.

Introduction

The Body Shop has built its international reputation on selling skin and hair care preparations, based on natural ingredients and formulas, available in a range of convenient sizes that meet the real needs of the consumer. The Body Shop stocks over 400 products, which have not been tested on animals and which are produced and sold with the minimum damage to the environment. It has also become known for promoting wider environmental issues, as a champion for human rights and as a leader in establishing fair trading schemes with developing countries.

By March 1994 The Body Shop had 1,100 shops in forty-five countries and was trading in nineteen languages. It had a larger presence abroad than any other British retailer. At the year end 28 February 1994, the group's turnover was £195.4 million, and its pre-tax profits were £29.7 million.

Growth and development

The first shop

The Body Shop's success has been achieved since 1976 when its founder, Anita Roddick, opened the first branch in Brighton. The first shop was opened on a budget of £4,000 and stocked just fifteen basic products. The products were displayed in cheap plastic bottles in five sizes, which allowed customers to buy as much or as little as they required. The bottles had handwritten labels which were liable to run if they became wet in the steamy atmosphere of a bathroom. The idea of a refill service was used to disguise the shortage of bottles. The traditional dark green that characterizes The Body Shop was initially used to cover up the damp patches on the walls of the shop, and The Body Shop's logo was designed for just £25.

The ideas for the initial products stemmed from Anita Roddick's travels into remote areas of the world where she had seen women using natural products for their skin and hair. She effectively transported this approach to the West and developed such products as Avocado Moisture Cream, Hawthorn Hand Cream, Cocoa Butter Body Lotion, and Seaweed and Birch Shampoo.

The first shop.

success

We care about humanising the business community we will continue to show that success and profits can go hand in hand with ideals and values.
Money works, success talks ideals count and add meaning. Values matter and give purpose.

The Body Shop's goals and values are as important as our products and our profits.
The Body Shop has soul – don't lose it!

humanity

We care about our customers and will continue to bring humanity into the marketplace.
Be good traders – sell well but give care and attention.

values

We enbrace everyone who wooks for The Body Shop and with The Body Shop as part of our extended family. We are all the Company: it is up to us all to make it work.
Enter into the spirit of partnership. We're all in this together.

family

The Body Shop Charter

The Body Shop Charter exists to record what we are and what we do: all individuals are empowered to contribute in their own way, and to help turn The Body Shop vision of making the world a better place into a reality.

We will continue to create products which show that we care: by not testing on animals, by using naturally based ingredients that are close to source, by making products which work for our customers. *Products affect more than skin and hair. Our vital ingredients? Honesty and responsibility.*

create

Our policies and our products are geared to meet the real needs of real people, both inside and outside the company.
Know ourselves: know our customers. Stay real!

real

Honesty, integrity and caring form the foundations of the Company, and should flow through everything we do. Be true to yourself and others .Tell no lies. Open your heart and mind. Be direct.

integrity

respecting

We will demonstrate out care for the world in which we live, by respecting fellow human beings, by not harming animals, by working to conserve our planet.
We are all interconnected. Live together or die alone!

We care about each other as individuals: we will continue to endeavour to bring meaning and pleasure to the workplace.
Treat everyone equally. Break down barriers. Build mutual trust and respect.

care

challenge

We will continue to search, to challenge, to question, to celebrate life and generate joy and excitement.
Re–examine all you've been told... Smile. Laugh. Enjoy!

The Body Shop Charter.

Anita Roddick's simple formula was to provide a straightforward product without the heavy advertising and expensive packaging of the mainstream cosmetics industry. It worked; the shop took £130 on its first day of trading and continued to go from strength to strength.

Expansion through franchising

Most of the expansion has been achieved by franchising new shops to people who share the same values as The Body Shop, namely 'profit with responsibility', especially towards their customers, staff, the environment, human rights and trading with developing countries. These shared values are clearly stated in the Body Shop charter, shown on the left.

	No. of shops: Feb 92	No. of shops: Feb 93	No. of shops: Apr 94	First shop opening
Antigua	1	1	1	1987
Australia	38	43	48	1983
Austria	7	8	9	1986
Bahamas	4	4	3	1985
Bahrain	1	1	1	1985
Belgium	6	8	11	1978
Bermuda	1	1	1	1987
Brunei			1	1993
Canada	92	104	107	1980
Cayman Islands	1	1	1	1989
Cyprus	1	1	1	1983
Denmark (inc. Faroes)	7	11	15	1981
DFDS (ferries)			4	1993
Finland	11	15	17	1981
France	10	16	26	1982
Germany	33	37	43	1983
Gibraltar	1	1	1	1988
Greece	16	23	31	1979
Hong Kong	8	8	9	1984
Iceland	1	2	2	1980
Indonesia	1	2	4	1990
Italy	29	37	39	1984
Japan	3	11	27	1990
Kuwait	1	2	2	1986
Luxemburg	1	2	2	1991
Macau			1	1993
Malaysia	10	10	12	1984
Malta	1	1	1	1987
Mexico			2	1993
The Netherlands	27	40	47	1982
New Zealand	5	7	9	1989
Norway	14	15	14	1985
Oman	2	2	2	1986
Portugal	5	8	8	1986
Qatar	1	1	1	1987
Republic of Ireland	6	10	10	1981
Saudi Arabia	8	10	16	1987
Singapore	8	11	9	1983
Spain	23	33	54	1986
Sweden	32	34	43	1979
Switzerland	19	19	21	1983
Taiwan	3	5	7	1988
Thailand			2	1993
UAE	1	2	4	1983
USA	78	120	177	1988
International	517	667	846	
UK and Channel Islands	210	233	239	1976
GRAND TOTAL	727	900	1085	

The growth of The Body Shop.

Essentially, a franchised shop is independently owned and run by the franchisee. The franchise is a contractual licence granted by the franchiser, which in this case is The Body Shop. It allows the franchisee to operate his or her Body Shop to the same standards and format as all the other units in the franchised chain. In the early 1990s franchises were costing around £200,000. The deal included the use of the corporate name and the opportunity to stock the products, and also covered shop fittings, design and legal fees. By expanding in this way, The Body Shop shared the costs of its expansion with its franchisees. This allowed for a far more rapid penetration into other areas of the UK and abroad.

The first franchises were offered in 1977 through a less formalized self-financing scheme, and this led to the opening of shops in Bognor Regis and Hove.

International developments

In 1978 The Body Shop went international and opened up its first branch in Belgium. This was followed by shops in Sweden in 1979 and Canada in 1980. By 1983 it had got as far as Australia, and in 1988 the first United States branch of The Body Shop opened in New York. By 1993 a branch of The Body Shop was opening somewhere in the world every two and a half days.

The development of the Single European Market has allowed The Body Shop to capitalize on its considerable presence in Europe. It has enabled the company to grant further franchises and has facilitated the movement of goods and services from England to its existing European franchises. The rapid worldwide growth of the Body Shop can be clearly seen from the table on the left.

Going public

In 1984 The Body Shop became a public company with 5 million shares floated on the unlisted securities market of the Stock Exchange. There was a tremendous reception for the shares, which has been maintained with a continued sound performance at the Stock Exchange. This has helped to finance the company's growth, including the construction of manufacturing and warehouse facilities and the development of various subsidiary companies. One such company is 'Colourings', which The Body Shop launched in 1986 to provide a line of cosmetics. This product line was extended in 1990 to include a range of cosmetics developed for all skin tones.

The general role of marketing

The Body Shop obviously has a unique approach to marketing. Before we analyse it in detail it is important to clarify certain general points about the marketing function.

The marketing function

Business organizations consider the marketing function to involve:

1   the identification of consumer needs;
2   the satisfaction of those needs in such a way as to yield a profit, while also encouraging consumers to make further purchases and to recommend the products and services of the organization.

The marketing mix

In the majority of business organizations, someone (or in a large organization usually an entire department) takes responsibility for all the various activities associated with marketing. These involve matching the **product** to consumer needs, determining the **price**, deciding upon where and how the product or service should be **placed** (distributed) in the market and **promoting** it through publicity, advertising and sales techniques. These activities are known as the four Ps, or ingredients, of marketing and are elaborated upon in the table below.

PRODUCT	PRICE
• Differentiating the product from its competitors by creating a brand image using a special type of packaging, providing after-sales service, and developing special features of quality and reliability. • Providing packaging to give information, act as protection, allow the product to act as a gift, and minimize possible environmental damage. • Updating, modifying or finding new products in acknowledgement of their limited life cycle. • Conducting a SWOT analysis to identify strengths, weaknesses, opportunities and threats facing the organization and its products.	• Setting a price that reflects the organization's objectives, the price elasticity of demand for the product, the organization's costs and competitors' prices. • The pricing method used may be based on cost-plus, target profit, perceived value or market rate.
PLACE	**PROMOTION**
• Deciding on where and how the product should be distributed. This is in terms of location and the possible use of a wholesaler, direct selling to a retailer, mail order or using a marketing board. • Keeping distribution costs to a competitive level. • Using a method of distribution that enhances the consumer's perception of the product.	• Stimulating and enforcing a need in the consumer. • Communicating information to the consumer about the type of product or service available and the quality of the product or service. • Selecting appropriate means of promoting the company such as advertising, public relations, creating a corporate image through brochures, logos and letterheads or offering competitions and free gifts.

Marketing activities

The marketing department develops an appropriate marketing strategy. This involves identifying what are considered to be the most important ingredients of the marketing operation, and hence determining the best marketing mix of the four Ps.

Ultimately, the marketing mix will depend upon the organization's business objectives. For example, the organization may decide that it should attempt to increase its market share. It may determine that this objective is best achieved by concentrating more upon lowering price and increasing its sales outlets. The organization may conclude that this strategy would require less attention to particular features of the products and would allow a saving on certain promotional activities.

The target market

The make-up of the marketing mix will depend upon the target market. A producer cannot expect to provide a range of products or services with sufficient variation to satisfy all the customers that make up the market as a whole. The producer must first decide on which market segment to aim for. The segment that offers the best prospects of achieving its objectives will then become its target market. The company's marketing strategy will therefore be to identify and satisfy the needs of a clearly defined set of customers.

Market information

Successfully identifying the target market and developing an appropriate strategy depends upon researching accurate information about the market.

Market research is not only concerned with the investigation into the consumer market for products. It also involves the creation of an original concept for a new or improved product, the analysis of existing or new methods of distribution, the sales organization, advertising and other promotional activities. The most important areas for the collection of market information are set out in the following table.

PRODUCT RESEARCH
- Testing features of design, materials or ingredients, colour, durability, ease of handling, fitness for purpose, reliability, operating capacity and quality of packaging.
- Psychological testing of reaction to brand name or perceived status or prestige associated with the purchase of the product.
- Comparable testing of competitors' products.

SALES AND DISTRIBUTION
- Measuring the effectiveness of the sales force in terms of the number and cost of calls and the number and size of orders.
- Evaluating different methods of distribution such as mail order, using a wholesaler or direct selling.
- Comparing marketing techniques by competitors.

PROMOTION AND ADVERTISING
- Measuring the effectiveness of advertising campaigns and promotional activities in terms of additional sales and the reaction of potential consumers.

ECONOMIC AND BUSINESS
- Forecasting the future behaviour of the economic, political and social variables that may influence the demand for the company's product and its position in the market.
- Investigating the sector of the economy in which the organization's activities fall and in particular the activities of its competitors, suppliers and trade customers.
- Evaluating social and demographic trends such as the size and structure of the population, the rate of household formation and social stratification.

CONSUMER RESEARCH
- Assessing the needs of consumers in the context of changing tastes and preferences.
- Evaluating the potential for new, improved or existing products.
- Researching the background of consumers in terms of sex, marital status, family size, socio-economic class, and age.
- Conducting surveys relating to psychological factors such as image, social standing and personal values and how they influence consumer behaviour.
- Evaluating different channels of distribution.

Types of market information.

Market information is generally gathered through two forms of research activity: desk research and field research.

Desk research

Desk research involves the gathering of information from existing publications. A useful range of publications stems from the Government Statistical Office. These provide data on general economic and social change.

They may be supplemented by trade publications, which are produced on behalf of firms that constitute an industry or a particular trade. These trade journals contain data, information and articles on subjects and developments of relevance to the industry as a whole.

The individual company's own records of past sales may provide valuable data for research purposes: for example, establishing a connection between the company's own performance and outside influences identified as possible reasons for fluctuations in sales.

Field research

Field research may be used to supplement the general trends identified through the desk research. It will provide a more detailed analysis of the factors that eventually lead the consumer to select purchases from the choice available.

Direct contact is normally established with the consumer through an appropriate questionnaire, which is then used with a representative sample of the total market. The sample should be selected in such a way that it reproduces the characteristics of the total consumer group. This may be best achieved by selecting the sample randomly or taking a quota, or by setting up a panel of typical consumers to report on key consumer issues. The questionnaire itself may then be conducted through personal interview, setting up a discussion group, or through a postal or telephone survey.

The Body Shop's approach to marketing
A unique approach to marketing

In her autobiography, *Body and Soul*, Anita Roddick, the founder of The Body Shop, justifies the organization's unique approach to marketing:

> The essential dilemma for the cosmetics industry can be easily explained. The big growth area is not in fragrance or make-up, but in skin care products, yet the simple truth is that such products can do nothing more than cleanse, polish and protect the skin and hair. That's it. Amen. End of story. There are no magic potions, no miracle cures, no rejuvenating creams. That is all hype and lies. . . .
>
> The trouble with marketing is that consumers are hyped out. The din of advertising and promotion has grown so loud that they can no longer tell one pitch from another and they are becoming cynical about the whole process. They have heard too many lies. What we have tried to do is establish credibility by educating our customers, giving them intelligent information about where ingredients come from, how they are tested and what they can be used for. It humanizes the company, making customers feel they are buying from people whose business practices they know and trust.

By adopting such a refreshingly honest approach to its customers, The Body Shop has been able to achieve two major objectives:

1 to establish a reputation as a quality provider of no-nonsense skin and hair care preparations, based on natural ingredients and available in a range of convenient sizes;

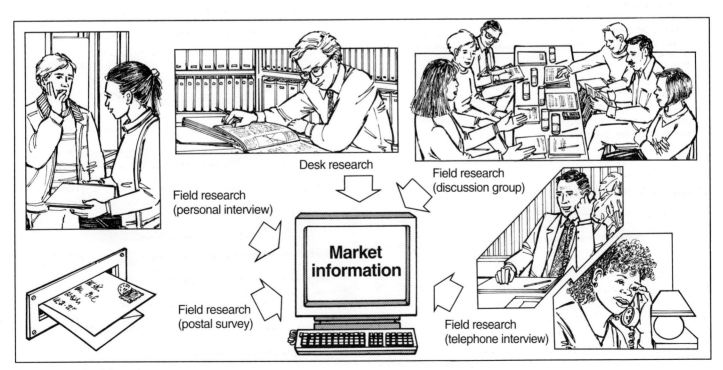

Field research (personal interview)

Desk research

Field research (discussion group)

Field research (postal survey)

Market information

Field research (telephone interview)

Gathering market information.

2   to establish a worldwide reputation as a values-led company.

The two objectives are clearly linked. Public relations activity has helped to link the name of The Body Shop with a genuine concern for human rights, the environment, animal rights, and fair trading with developing countries. This in turn has helped The Body Shop to convince its customers of the integrity and quality of its products. Consequently, members of its target market have come confidently into its shops, as they have opened, and marketing activities continue within that environment. They largely involve providing very accurate information about the range of existing products or the properties of new ones.

The Body Shop has never had a formal marketing department or an advertising budget. It prefers to promote its products as part of its wider social and environmental activities.

Target market

When she started trading through The Body Shop, Anita Roddick unwittingly anticipated the development of a growing niche market for no-nonsense green products. In going for this market she targeted a group of women who had previously been ignored by the cosmetics industry. They wanted products with benign ingredients produced by a company run by women and with an understanding of women. She recognized that this group did not necessarily want to buy cosmetics always in large quantities or in expensive containers and packaging. There was a growing demand for cosmetics to be sold in a range of sizes with the minimum of packaging. There was a need for a shop with a classless, friendly but essentially stylish image, a shop that favoured an 'enlightened capitalist' approach, that traded ethically and did not wish to damage the environment or abuse human or animal rights. In trying to meet the needs of this target group, Anita Roddick developed a marketing strategy that clearly reflects the four Ps.

Product

The means by which The Body Shop creates the right product to meet consumer needs can be clearly seen from the figure on the right.

Market information

The Body Shop has always entered into a close dialogue with its customers in order to identify their needs. This has been at an informal level between customers and staff, or more formally when customers have been encouraged to express their views through in-store activities such as card surveys.

Researching new ingredients

The Body Shop's New Product Development Department conducts extensive laboratory research into new ingredients to discover whether they are suitable for the basis of products. Many of these ingredients may have been suggested by Anita Roddick as a result of her travels overseas and observations of the customs and cultures of people abroad. Alternatively they may be based on ideas that have been handed down from one generation to another in this country.

The laboratory research into all these natural preparations based on fruits or flowers will lead to the development of products that are safe, look good and have a pleasant smell. For example, extensive research showed that it was possible to produce a number of hair preparations from bananas.

Creating the right product.

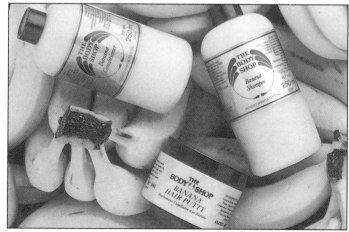

Banana hair products.

Testing for quality

Product development involves testing. The Body Shop neither tests nor commissions the testing of any product or ingredient on animals, and uses no ingredients that have been tested on animals within the last five years. To ensure product safety and quality, The Body Shop carried out controlled testing on human volunteers, and employs various technological alternatives, such as computer models for microbiological analyses.

Product market evaluation

The findings from the various tests on the new product idea are incorporated into an overall market evaluation. This includes consideration of the costs of the production process and the ingredients. Over 90 per cent of new product ideas are rejected at this stage. Only the very best go forward.

Consumer testing

This is carried out within the shops. Generally it involves sending a number of test bottles out with a questionnaire. Customers are asked to try out the new product and record their responses to a number of standard questions. These are worded to elicit information about how and where customers might use the new preparation and how effective they have found it. The question that would really determine whether The Body Shop has developed a winning product is obviously: 'Would you be prepared to buy it?'.

Production control

To ensure that the final product is of the highest possible quality, The Body Shop produces it using a highly computerized process. For example, in making fruit-based shampoos the computer checks the weight of each ingredient and precisely controls the water levels and the temperature. The shampoos go through a mixing process for about seven hours. Throughout the production process a sophisticated quality control system operates which tests each batch of product.

To maintain quality, constant checks and scientific tests are carried out on all products. For example, oils and perfumes are subjected to heat tests to ensure that their characteristics of smell and consistency do not change at different temperatures.

Packaging

The simplicity of The Body Shop packaging and the product information on it help to differentiate Body Shop products still further from those of its competitors. The bottles used by some companies appear to be more expensive than their contents. The packaging used by The Body Shop clearly reflects company values, since many products are sold in bottles made of recyclable plastic. By the beginning of 1992, The Body Shop was able to recycle 1 tonne of high density polyethylene per week. The Body Shop also encourages its customers to return clean, empty bottles for refill. Between 1991 and 1992, 560,000 bottles were refilled. Its attitude towards waste management is clearly reflected in one of its leaflets, shown opposite

Price

The Body Shop's pricing policy is very different from that of its major competitors. It reflects fundamentally different business objectives. Whereas most of its competitors are concerned with maximizing profits, The Body Shop has wider social, environmental, and human rights objectives. Anita Roddick clearly expressed this in her autobiography when she wrote:

WASTE

The Body Shop's approach to waste management is simple: reduce, reuse, recycle (in that order). Disposal is a last resort.

Waste - solid or liquid - can have a huge potential impact on the environment if managed improperly. When we commissioned an Environmental Review in 1989 it highlighted two particular areas in need of improvement in our business. We now have well developed recycling schemes and a wastewater treatment facility.

Waste Plastic

The most important things we do to reduce solid waste are to avoid excessive packaging, refill empty product containers and make packaging out of readily recycled materials.

The Body Shop produced 32 million bottles and caps in 1991. Generating so much plastic, we are aware of the impact this could have on the planet. That's why we offer alternatives to lobbing out the bottles with the garbage.

THINK REFILL!

The Refill Bar

Our Refill Bar is probably the most important environmental service we offer in our shops. When customers bring back their clean, empty containers we will refill them with fresh product at a discount. This cuts down on plastic packaging and saves money.

The Body Shop and waste management.

Along with the profit and loss sheets, I would want to know about the profit and loss for the environment, or the community or the Third World.

This means that, for The Body Shop, pricing is not a matter of assessing what the market will take. Nor is it a question of marking-up a cosmetic item to reflect the consumer's inflated perceived value, or having to price a product at a high level to cover the advertising expenses, expensive packaging and distribution costs. The Body Shop has none of this; its items are priced on what is essentially a cost-plus basis. The price has to cover the development of the ingredients and products, its sale and distribution to the franchisee and in turn their mark-up. There is no money spent on advertising, and packaging is kept to a minimum. Consequently, the consumer is only asked to pay for the product, basic distribution costs and a mark-up. Because of its pricing policy the demand for The Body Shop's products is relatively price-inelastic. Consumers see them as quality products, which are good value for money, and which have the added value of providing support for causes relating to social, environmental and human rights issues. They are unlikely to be persuaded to buy cheaper substitutes.

Place

The Body Shop attaches a great deal of importance to the making of decisions about where to locate its outlets and how to distribute its products. Its Development Team is constantly searching for new sites. By studying the demographics, income distribution and shopping trends within certain regions of a country it is possible to target particular towns or cities. Suitable locations will then be identified by studying pedestrian traffic flows. Because of The Body Shop's policy of not advertising, and because the average sale per customer is under £10, it needs a location that will attract large numbers of customers with an appropriate level of disposable income.

Once the site has been identified, the desired image must be created for the shop. This will help to enhance the consumer's perception of the products. Customers are attracted into the shop by the scent and they are entertained and educated by its windows. The shop assistants are trained to treat customers as potential friends. They are instructed to be helpful, to be honest about the products and to offer advice but not to apply aggressive selling techniques. The simple, cheerful product displays and the availability of masses of product information are intended to allow the products to sell themselves and create a pleasurable shopping experience.

The distribution chain is from manufacturer to warehouse and then on to individual shops or out through mail order.

Promotion

The Body Shop's promotional activities are based on the principle of identifying a real cosmetic need and then attempting to satisfy it. This means that it is not necessary to create demand through spending money on advertising, but rather to promote the product in the context of the need.

For example, the introduction of the London Marathon and resultant complaints of sore feet by competitors prompted the Body Shop to develop a Peppermint Foot Lotion. This was made from a modern version of an old recipe. Essentially it involved peppermint, menthol and arnica, with almond oil, cocoa butter and lanolin. It had the properties to soothe tired feet, soften hard skin and inhibit foot odour. The Body Shop secured the permission of the organizers to hand out free samples of the lotion to all the competitors in the London Marathon. This promotional activity was covered by all the national newspapers and gave far more publicity to The Body Shop than an expensive advertising campaign might have done.

The Body Shop's policy of active campaigning also has a promotional effect. It helps to raise the profile of the company, attracting a great deal of media attention and so bringing more potential customers into the shops. For example, The Body Shop joined with Amnesty International in a campaign to raise awareness of human rights violations around the world. The Body Shop campaign involved window posters and leaflets and successfully increased the membership of Amnesty International by over 1,000.

Indirectly, the values and issues that The Body Shop promotes help to encourage more customers to come into the shops. This is because they are made to feel that their purchase is indirectly supporting each particular cause, or sometimes more directly supporting it. For example, Brazil Nut Conditioner aids the Kayapo Indians in their fight to save their homeland in the Amazonian rainforest: by producing brazil nut oil, they are guaranteed an income which will help them to protect their land rights.

The Body Shop prides itself on its ability to communicate information to the consumer about the type of product or service available and its quality. This is achieved by supporting each new product when it goes out to the shops with a pack that provides staff with information about the product, instructions

Examples of Body Shop campaign leaflets.

on display, and what to put in the window. The Body Shop also pays a great deal of attention to the training of its staff. They are given basic training in hair care, skin types, raw ingredients and massage. They are also encouraged to try out new products. All of this helps them to speak with some authority when dealing with customers.

Activities

Short-answer questions

1 Give five reasons for The Body Shop's success in the market for skin and hair treatments.
2 Outline the major differences in marketing strategy between The Body Shop and its competitors.
3 How has The Body Shop managed to maintain a consistent quality of service throughout all of its outlets?
4 How does The Body Shop identify consumer needs?
5 How does The Body Shop differentiate its products from those of its competitors?

6 Identify The Body Shop's target market.
7 What is Anita Roddick's view of the marketing function?
8 How does The Body Shop convince its customers of the integrity and quality of its products?
9 Discuss the view that The Body Shop's concern for the environment will ultimately lead to an increase in its market share?
10 Analyse the view that The Body Shop is a high profile company which has achieved its success through its founder's clever use of promotional activities.

Case study

The following article about a Body Shop promotion appeared on the front page of The Independent, *12 July 1993.*

Task

Explain how the activities of the Sunscreen Spray Patrol clearly reflect The Body Shop's fundamental marketing strategy.

Sunscreen soldiers on parade as part of a 'be safe under the sun' campaign that is targeting those baring arms and risking skin cancer

Hoping to turn the health tide, the spray patrol marching along the seafront yesterday. They met a mixed response: 'I didn't come here to be sprayed with that stuff,' said one holidaymaker

Photograph: Edward Sykes

The Brighton beach patrols go for the burn

A DAY by the seaside was never meant to be like this. Sunscreen spray patrols made their first appearance yesterday on a British beach, warning the public that unprotected sunbathing can cause skin cancers, *writes Roger Tredre.*

Holiday-makers on the front at Brighton were puzzled by the teams of young men and women, dressed in red T-shirts, black shorts and spotted bandanas, who offered sunbathers free squirts of watermelon sunscreen.

The campaign, launched by the Body Shop with Brighton Borough Council and the East Sussex Health Authority, is inspired by Australia's 'Slip, Slop, Slap' spray patrols and beach 'mole-check' centres.

Avalee Chapman, 26, who was running a 'spray station' on the beach opposite the Grand Hotel, said: 'You tell them to close their mouths, make sure they're upwind of you, and let them have it.'

Spray patrols are planned in Torquay, Blackpool and Great Yarmouth this summer. They could become as familiar a feature of the British seaside as ice-cream sellers and deck-chair attendants.

The Body Shop Survey

THE BODY SHOP

Name ....

Address ....
....
.... Tel ....
....

How would you describe your experience at our shop today?

❏ Fantastic ❏ Great ❏ Good ❏ Not great ❏ Pretty bad

Were you disappointed with anything? ❏ Yes ❏ No

If yes, was it any of the following?

❏ The service   ❏ The mood in the shop

❏ The products   ❏ The information material

❏ Other (please specify) ....
....
....

Which types of products have you bought at The Body Shop in the past year?

❏ For yourself ❏ For a family member ❏ As a gift

What is most important to you about The Body Shop?

❏ Products ❏ Company values ❏ Convenience

What skin and hair care products do you NOT purchase from The Body Shop? And where do you buy them from?
....
....

Is there any product that you would like to see us carry?
....
....

How often do you shop at The Body Shop?

❏ At least once a month   ❏ Several times a year
❏ Once or twice a year   ❏ Less than once a year
❏ This is my first visit to The Body Shop

Tell us a bit about yourself :

❏ I am a woman   ❏ I am a man
❏ I live in this city/town ❏ I have children at home
❏ I work outside the home   ❏ I am a student

I am . . . ❏ under 20 ❏ 21-30 ❏ 31-40 ❏ over 40

Can we contact you later to talk some more? ❏ Yes ❏ No
Would you like to receive our catalogue? ❏ Yes ❏ No

Thanks for taking the time to talk to us!

March 1993

A Body Shop survey card.

Local investigation

One of The Body Shop's survey cards is reproduced above. Study it carefully and then complete the following tasks.

Tasks

1 Analyse the extent to which the format, structure and language used in the survey reflects the image that The Body Shop would like to convey to its customers.
2 How might The Body Shop make use of the market information provided by the survey?
3 Identify the probable costs associated with organizing and conducting the survey.
4 Compare these costs with those that might have been incurred if the survey had been conducted by an independent market research company.
5 Comment on the statistical limitations of conducting the survey within the shops.
6 In groups of four, design a suitable questionnaire and conduct a survey within your school or college to identify the following:
    (a) the extent to which students in different sex and age groups are purchasing The Body Shop's products;
    (b) the most popular range of The Body Shop's products purchased by different sex and age groups;
    (c) the average expenditure per student, per month, on The Body Shop's products, also classified according to age and sex.

The class should combine its results and invite the manager of the nearest outlet of The Body Shop into the school or college to comment on the general findings and conclusions.

Media analysis 1

The Mostly Men range of products.

Tasks

1 Obtain promotional material that provides information on The Body Shop's Mostly Men Product Range.
2 Collect similar product information produced by The Body Shop's major competitors.
3 Produce a report on The Body Shop's range for men which analyses the following:
   (a) target market;
   (b) product range;
   (c) product information;
   (d) price;
   (e) special selling features.
   Wherever possible draw comparisons with The Body Shop's major competitors.

Media analysis 2

The article below appeared in The Independent, *31 July 1993.*

Tasks

1 What was the basis of The Body Shop's libel action?
2 How did the Channel 4 programme damage The Body Shop commercially?
3 Hold a class debate on the judge's summing up when he asked the jury to consider 'whether a businessman may undertake good works out of sheer altruism while at the same time recognizing – and this may be part of his motive – that good works are good for business'.
4 In the light of The Body Shop's marketing strategy why was it essential for Anita Roddick to take libel action against Channel 4 and Fulcrum Productions?

Channel 4 sought to depict a 'cynical mask'. Anita and Gordon Roddick said its programme was a smear. **Marianne Macdonald** reports

Roddick libel claim lands a body blow

It may have been the holier-than-thou image of the Body Shop which prompted the makers of *Dispatches* to attack an empire which had long prided itself on helping the homeless, the environment, the community and the Third World. It may have been the additional fact of its healthy profits. Either way, the onslaught proved disastrous.

'Tonight's Dispatch examines the Body Shop phenomenon, with its founders Anita and Gordon Roddick. Does their claim to be different really stand up to a full body search?' the 45-minute programme on Channel 4 demanded in May last year. The makers saw it as puncturing a cynical mask to reveal greed and hypocrisy beneath. The Body Shop saw it as a degrading and inaccurate smear and, for the first time in its 17 years, sued for libel.

For Anita Roddick, the case was crucial. She and her husband had built their £365m empire on 'conviction merchandising'. Vociferous campaigns helped pull in customers by persuading them they were not just being frivolous when they bought dewberry body lotion, but somehow helping the planet.

The windows of its 950 stores world-wide displayed slogans for human rights and international issues. From the start its cosmetics – such as banana hair putty, orchid oil cleansing milk and Viennese facial chalk – were sold in unadorned, refillable bottles which conserved resources and cut waste. Staff were encouraged to participate in community projects. Annual reports announced the company had sent more than 60 volunteers to Romania and recycled vast quantities of consumer waste.

Anita and Gordon Roddick said they fought Channel 4 because the programme had cynically challenged their sincere belief that business could be altruistic. Expecting a balanced picture, the Body Shop gave Fulcrum Productions, the film makers, full co-operation. Mr Roddick told the High Court: 'It gave the impression we were dishonest, deceitful in everything we did.'

The programme was repeated three days later. As a result of hostile reaction, profits fell by 4 per cent, the jury was told.

The libels in the programme centred around claims that the Body Shop pledge not to use ingredients until five years after they had been animal-tested was largely worthless, partly because many new ingredients took that long to gain approval for use. The makers also alleged they were misleading customers by labelling products 'Not tested on animals' and 'Against animal testing'.

The programme claimed other companies, such as Boots and Sainsbury, adopted more stringent criteria preferred by the RSPCA under which they refused to use ingredients which had been animal-tested after a fixed date. These chains' products, it said, were substantially cheaper than the Body Shop's.

It also falsely claimed the company had launched a petition opposing an EC directive on product-testing on animals in a bid to prop up its share price even though the directive had already been withdrawn. Further, that the Body Shop had broken promises made when it opened a soap factory in Easterhouse, Glasgow, that a quarter of the profits would go to the local community.

The Body Shop rebutted the allegations. Charles Gray QC argued few customers beyond the 'odd 14- or 15-year-old girl' could be misled by explanations of its animal testing policies in its leaflets; that the 'five-year rule' was supported by the British Union for the Abolition of Vivisection, and strictly applied; that even the House of Lords had been unaware of the abandonment of the EC directive. As for the Easterhouse claims, the company had donated £50,000 to the area despite the factory making losses of around £130,000 in 1990 and 1991.

Summing up, Mr Justice Jowitt asked the jury to consider 'whether a businessman may undertake good works out of sheer altruism while at the same time recognising – and this may be part of his motive – that good works are good for business'.

Cynical commercialism or a true ideology? Or could the two go hand in hand? The jury thought so and, for Channel 4 and Fulcrum Productions, their *Body Search* had proved more like a body blow.

Introduction

International Computers Limited (ICL) is one of Europe's leading computer systems and services companies. It operates in over eighty countries and has about 24,000 employees. Within the UK it is the second largest supplier of information technology systems, with about 20 per cent of the UK market for business systems.

ICL is also the second largest information technology company in the Nordic region. The company has achieved a particularly strong position in both the retail and wholesale sectors. It is the world's third largest supplier of in-store retail information systems, in terms of numbers of systems installed, and the number one supplier of these systems in the UK, with about 37 per cent of the market. It is also number one in French hypermarkets and Italian department stores, and number one in DIY stores in the UK, USA, France, Australia and Sweden. ICL is also a leading supplier to central and local government both within the UK and abroad, and has a strong position in utilities, financial services, and transport and travel.

ICL is the third largest supplier of in-store information systems.

Growth and development

ICL was formed in 1968 through the successive merger of the UK's leading domestic computer suppliers, including English Electric Computers and International Computers and Tabulators (ICT). The merger was encouraged by the Industrial Reorganisation Corporation, which was set up by the government of the time to hasten, in various sectors, the creation of companies that would be large enough to compete in international markets. The government was particularly concerned about companies in areas of new and high technology, where expenditure on research and development was vital for competitiveness and where smaller companies would experience problems in funding large-scale programmes. In the interests of the economy as a whole, they also wanted to avoid a wasteful duplication of effort.

In 1984, ICL was acquired by the UK telecommunications company STC (formerly Standard Telephone and Cable), and this produced one of Europe's leading communications and information systems groups. At the end of 1990 the Japanese company Fujitsu invested in ICL by taking an 80 per cent shareholding in the company, with STC (now owned by Northern Telecom of Canada) retaining a 20 per cent shareholding. Since then, ICL has operated as an autonomous company within the Fujitsu federation of companies. In 1991, ICL merged with Nokia Data of Finland, the leading information technology company in Scandinavia. Acquisitions and joint ventures involving companies from Europe, the United States and the Far East are also very important features of the growth and development of ICL. The company sees Europe as its domestic market and plans to be the leading supplier in its chosen markets in Europe by the mid-1990s. Its corporate objectives are to increase turnover and market share in this part of the world through a policy of acquisitions, mergers and joint ventures. In fact ICL's mission statement is 'to become Europe's leading information technology company by applying world class technology and people to understanding and satisfying our customer requirements'. As far as technology is concerned, ICL is a major investor, and in 1993 the company spent £209 million on research and development – equivalent to 10 per cent of its revenue.

As indicated in the mission statement, the future competitive position of ICL is also closely linked to the quality of its workforce, and this is shown by the significant investment that the company makes in its employees. In 1993, ICL spent £20 million on training and development programmes, and the quality of these programmes has been recognized by the Government, who selected the company for a series of National Training Awards. The National Training Awards competition is administered by the Employment Department. It recognizes exceptionally effective training by giving awards to organizations who can demonstrate that their investment in training has paid off in terms of improved performance.

In 1988, we submitted our Quality The ICL Way training programme. It was acknowledged by the National Training Council as 'the most outstanding and successful training carried out in the UK'.

We regard it as wholly innovative. It enabled us to bring about a complete culture change. It equipped all our people with the language and techniques of quality improvement. It set us on the road to our future.

The general approach to training as part of human resource management

An important aspect of human resource planning is the training of employees and the development of management and supervisory skills. The kinds of factors that oblige a company to review, modify and update its training and development programmes include the following:

1 an investment project requiring new skills because it involves new plant, machinery or equipment and the application of a new technology;
2 a decline in productivity, a fall-off in quality, increased scrap, breakdowns in machinery and a rise in customer complaints;
3 the introduction of new working methods that seek to trim down the number of employees in certain operations and require that the remaining employees adopt additional skills and generally agree to undertake a wider range of tasks and responsibilities;
4 alterations to the end product or service or some kind of diversification that affects working methods;
5 a need to raise the skills levels of existing employees because labour shortages make it difficult to recruit such skills from outside the company;
6 the promotion or transfer of management and supervisory staff and the need to develop their full potential;
7 a need to increase job satisfaction and motivation as part of a strategy to reduce labour turnover and absenteeism;
8 a need to improve upon working practices and methods in order to reduce the number of accidents and protect the health of the workforce;
9 legislation designed to protect the environment that has implications for existing methods of production.

Having set a budget for training a company must then ensure that it gets the best possible return on its investment in human capital. This means that the training needs must be correctly identified, the appropriate standard of skill established, the

training programme put together and correctly administered, and the results achieved by the trainees then compared with the standard of performance that they hoped to reach.

Training needs

In the case of improving or widening the existing skills of operators or craft workers, or of programmes for new employees, it will be necessary to carry out a skills analysis. This analysis produces a job description covering the physical and mental activities involved in various tasks, the knowledge needed, and the necessary standard of work measured by quality and volume of output. A machine-tool operator, for example, will need certain manual skills to set up and operate a machine and measuring instruments, an ability to read and interpret drawings and an ability to make certain judgements. The job analysis therefore covers not only the physical movements but also other aspects of the employee's behaviour relevant to the job. Human resource planning will also need to establish any longer term skill requirements because a forecast shortage of highly skilled employees may involve setting up apprenticeship schemes up to five years in advance.

Designing the training programme

The structure and content of the programme must ensure that employees acquire the necessary skills and knowledge and also develop the appropriate attitudes and behaviour relevant to the job. The programme design must also seek to motivate employees to complete the course and reach the required standard. This motivation factor may be provided by a pay increase or promotion, or by the status and satisfaction associated with possessing a new skill and using machinery and equipment with the most up-to-date technology. Employees must also recognize the relevance of the training, and the training methods used should also sustain their interest.

Motivation will suffer if employees develop a sense of failure or frustration at making only slow progress. Any complex tasks must therefore be broken down into a series of simpler operations so that trainees can learn and practise each stage separately until the desired level of productivity and quality is achieved. Employees can then move on to the next stage and the progress made will generate a sense of achievement and satisfaction. A series of stages can then be practised so that the

Occupation	Males* (%)	Females* (%)	All (%)
Managers and administrators	13.8	16.5	14.7
Professional	23.3	31.3	26.6
Associate professional and technical	20.0	26.8	23.5
Clerical and secretarial	14.0	12.3	12.7
Craft and related	11.3	5.3	10.5
Personal and protective	16.6	11.7	13.4
Sales	14.4	10.0	11.4
Plant and machine operatives	5.6	4.7	5.4
Other	6.5	4.9	5.7
All occupations	13.4	14.1	13.7

Employees receiving job-related training in the four weeks prior to the survey, by occupation, as a percentage of all employees. (Employees are all those of working age: 16–64 for men; 16–59 for women.)
Source: Labour Market Quarterly Review, August 1993.

Occupation	Received some on-the-job training (%)	Received some off-the-job training (%)	Training leads to qualification or credit (%)
Managers and administrators	36.7	75.6	32.2
Professional	40.5	73.0	32.7
Associate professional and technical	43.7	73.6	51.4
Clerical and secretarial	40.1	68.6	41.4
Craft and related	42.9	77.3	66.4
Personal and protective	46.5	67.1	56.6
Sales	43.3	66.0	52.5
Plant and machine operatives	47.9	59.0	45.5
Other	37.7	70.6	55.5
All occupations	41.6	71.4	45.0

Type of training received by employees, by occupation, as a percentage of all employees receiving training. (Employees are all those of working age: 16–64 for men; 16–59 for women.)
Source: Labour Market Quarterly Review, August 1993.

It is important that sufficient time is devoted to training.

standards reached in earlier ones can be maintained, and at the same time employees can also see the relevance of each part of the training as the whole task is put together. Any theoretical part of the training should be dealt with in a way that clearly shows its relevance to the skills being acquired or helps to explain the reason for developing certain attitudes or behaviour.

Once the content of the training programme is determined, a choice must be made between on-the-job training and off-the-job training.

On-the-job training

This is a common form of training when the task involved is not too complex and the relevant skills are not too difficult to acquire. The trainee is placed in the actual working environment and uses the same kinds of machinery, tools, equipment and materials as the fully productive worker. On-the-job training is also possible for certain kinds of clerical and administrative jobs where the trained will immediately handle the relevant paperwork or carry out certain procedures. This is a relatively inexpensive form of training as it does not need specialist facilities and the job is learned on the machinery and equipment to be used when the training period is completed. It avoids the problems that can arise when trainees are moved from the artificial environment of a training establishment, where skills and knowledge have been gained using different kinds of machinery and equipment.

The success of on-the-job training will depend heavily upon the teaching and communication skills of the instructor. This may be someone at supervisory level or an experienced employee still carrying out the job. The time that the instructor can devote to the trainee will be very important. There is also a risk that the trainee will learn to 'cut corners', and although some time-saving practices may not adversely affect the efficiency or health and safety of experienced workers, they may be inappropriate for trainees.

A lack of supervision and instruction during this kind of training may lead to a high proportion of scrapped work and possibly even damage to machinery and equipment. Workers sometimes make remarks, humorous or otherwise, that can undermine the confidence of trainees, leading to stress and hence a reduction in the rate of progress.

On-the-job training will be more successful as a way of acquiring what are mainly visible skills if the supervisor has completed an instructor's training course. In this case the supervisor will have developed instruction techniques, such as breaking a job down into separate stages and pointing out which of them needs special attention or where precautions need to be taken. The supervisor will also have been trained in the communication skills needed for dealing with trainees. This training will help the supervisor to answer questions clearly, explain working methods or procedures, give encouragement or correct mistakes, and generally motivate the trainee. A trained instructor will also learn to gauge the amount of supervision that a particular trainee needs, and to build up his or her confidence.

Off-the-job training

Many small companies will be restricted mainly to on-the-job training because their intake of new employees is usually too small to justify spending on specialist training facilities and full-time instructors. They may allocate on-the-job training to a supervisor or an experienced worker. An employee may be persuaded to take on such a role if provided with a financial incentive, a job title that raises his or her status, or a generous amount of time to carry out such responsibilities.

Where, however, the skills analysis of a job shows the need for a much higher level of training – involving the acquisition of complex manual skills, coordination of the senses, powers of judgement and knowledge – then small companies may use off-the-job training facilities offered by both public and private sector educational and training institutions. The training needs of these companies may also have been identified by the government-sponsored local Training and Enterprise Councils (TECs), who may then meet the costs of the training organization being used. These TECs may also help to finance company training for employees up to 24 years old by providing Training Credits. The value of these credits depends upon the level of training being supplied by the company and can also be used to help with the costs of internal training.

Large companies may use external part-time and block-release courses as part of their off-the-job training programmes.

HERTFORDSHIRE
TRAINING & ENTERPRISE COUNCIL

Training and Enterprise Councils seek to identify local training needs and agencies that can then supply the training.

But the size of their labour force, their annual intake of new workers and their financial resources can make it viable for them to set up their own specialist training facilities staffed by trained instructors. Off-the-job training allows much longer courses of instruction dealing with higher level skills. Trainees can systematically work through the various stages of their course to develop the appropriate manual skills, knowledge, attitudes and behaviour.

Some trainees, however, might experience some difficulty adapting from the college or training school environment, with its special machinery and equipment, when they move into their actual work place. Off-the-job training may therefore be supported by a period of on-the-job training so that trainees can adjust gradually to the specific needs of the job before becoming fully productive workers.

Management and supervisory development

An essential part of human resource planning is ensuring that there is always a ready supply of trained and experienced people who can be promoted to supervisory positions and higher levels of management. Apart from preparing people for promotion it is also important for the success and efficiency of a company that the potential of people holding existing positions of responsibility and authority is developed as fully as possible. The techniques used in the development of management and supervisory staff are less clear-cut than those used for other types of employees. In the case of a machine tool operator, for example, the manual skills and knowledge requirements that produce quality output and high productivity can be clearly identified and then incorporated into a training programme for new operators. Determining the requirements of successful managers, however, is more of a problem. It may be generally agreed that successful managers will be able to:

- initiate, control, coordinate and organize certain activities within the company;
- identify the causes of current or potential problems and introduce successful remedies or preventative measures;
- generally improve the performance of the area of work for which they are responsible.

The problem is in identifying the personal qualities and skills that allow a manager to carry out these activities successfully, determining their relative importance, and assessing them in individuals. A further problem exists in devising appropriate techniques for developing similar qualities and skills in others who are likely to benefit from a management development programme.

ICL and investing in people

ICL sees developing its people to their full potential as vital to the company's success. It is seen as a means of strengthening its competitive position, because the way in which it manages and develops its people will influence the extent to which it can attract and retain staff, or lose them to its competitors. ICL has a flexible approach to such development so that it can identify different strengths and place individuals in roles where they can excel.

> We are a people Company. Our main strength lies in the quality and skill of the people who work here. So real progress will come about only by consistently developing and improving our skills. Development of this kind – people development – is one of the basic requirements for business success.
>
> 'The ICL Way' (a guide to ICL)

In 1989, ICL introduced a programme called 'Investing in People', which was based upon the company-wide application of certain requirements and processes concerning the management of people. One of the elements of this programme was called 'Developing Individual Capability', and this had four important aims:

1. to support the competitive position of the company by continuously increasing the capability of the staff;
2. to provide qualified and effective people to replace those who are promoted or transferred;
3. to develop fully the potential of all employees, so that they can make the best use their particular capabilities;
4. to motivate employees by allowing them to increase their area of responsibility and enjoy greater job satisfaction and earning power.

ICL and performance appraisal

ICL recognizes that the focal point for developing the capability of its employees is the relationship between employee and manager, including the appraisal process. Fair and objective feedback plays a vital part in personal development and improved performance. This requires a clear and unbiased assessment of each employee's effectiveness and requires detached judgements to be made. Employees are encouraged to view their development as a partnership with their manager involving regular discussions and agreed actions. The discussions and interviews that make up the appraisal process will provide management with important information relating to such issues as performance improvement, training planning, career development, salary review, succession planning, human resource planning and skills planning.

In ICL, formal appraisal and the completion of the appraisal form take place annually, but discussion between managers and their staff covering performance, objectives, career development and training are ongoing, with reviews occurring at least once a quarter. The annual formal appraisal is a documented summary and covers the following:

- a review of performance against objectives over the previous year;
- an assessment of an employee's particular strengths and weaknesses based upon key criteria which are important for the job;
- a Personal/Job Improvement Plan;
- a Career Development Plan;
- a Performance Rating;
- comments from the employee and the reviewing manager;
- agreement or reconfirmation of the objectives for the next year.

It is particularly important that the appraisal examines the extent to which an employee has reached certain objectives agreed at an earlier meeting. ICL sees these objectives as covering three areas:

1 **key results areas** – these deal with how employees can contribute to the business objectives of their own particular unit;
2 **performance standards** – these are objectives that will contribute to an improvement in the performance of the employee's own job;
3 **personal development** – objectives relating to increasing the knowledge or skills of an employee.

The company would expect each of the three types of objective to have a different emphasis. In the case of a new employee, for example, a heavy emphasis would be placed upon personal development objectives. An administrator responsible for operating processes may have the emphasis upon performance standards. A Director will have objectives almost totally concerned with key result areas.

ICL requires that objectives should be SMART – Specific, Measurable, Agreed, Realistic and Time-related. They must have a way of measuring the extent to which the various objectives have been achieved. ICL expects a manager to negotiate six to eight objectives with staff members, who should then commit themselves to the objectives.

Appraisal, therefore, is vital to many aspects of ICL's 'Investing in People' programme. In particular, that aspect of the programme directed at 'Developing Individual Capability' will be supported by those parts of the appraisal discussions which result in the following three plans.

A Personal/Job Improvement Plan

This recognizes that all employees can improve performance. The plan deals with areas for improvement or the need to respond to new demands in the job. The appraisal will have involved an analysis of the employee's strengths and weaknesses, and these will have been measured against the key criteria for the job or planned changes in the job content.

Career Development Plan

This helps to identify the most suitable job progression for the employee. Employees plan with their manager those actions that help to move them towards an aiming point in their career. Career development will take account of the aims of employees, but they must be realistic and reflect the needs of the business.

Career development options are not just concerned about promotions and may include progression within a career structure, secondment or sideways moves inside or outside an employee's existing unit to extend their experience. In many roles a wide experience is important for both career development and job improvement. If employees stay in their current role then discussions will seek ways of increasing job satisfaction.

Training Plan

Some of the needs relating to performance improvement and career development can be satisfied by formal training away from the place of work and aimed at developing the necessary level of knowledge, skill and attitudes. This training plan should also take account of training requirements at departmental level or company level.

In some companies the introduction of an appraisal scheme can often meet with much resistance from line managers who see it as too time-consuming. They do not agree with the view that everyone who has people reporting to them can make a contribution to the training function. Some might argue that they have a close working relationship with their staff, know who is doing well and who needs training and the appraisal interview is therefore unnecessary.

In ICL, however, the responsibility for developing individual capability is shared between the manager, the employee and the company. For the manager the development of people is seen as being just as important as meeting operational or financial objectives. It is the responsibility of managers to stimulate improved performance from their staff and to develop them in the broader interests of the company, because it is ICL's aim to fill as many vacancies as possible through the development of their existing employees.

Formal qualifications and external management development courses

As far as formal qualifications are concerned, those at supervisory or management level can be encouraged to study for the award of the relevant professional or institutional body. This is a particularly useful route for employees who are singled out for their first supervisory or management position, as it will be a valuable way of increasing their knowledge of the specialist area of work in which they are involved. In the case, however, of appointments to much higher positions, less attention is generally paid to additional formal qualifications. This is because these more experienced employees will already have demonstrated their in-depth knowledge in their specialist area of work. Formal qualifications in management itself are increasingly provided by universities, business schools, colleges and private management centres. These are valuable in so far as they can provide training in the clearly identifiable tools of management such as forecasting techniques, methods of cost analysis, work study and project management. They also provide training in specialist areas such as marketing, accountancy and human resource management, and encourage an appreciation of the factors that influence the business environment in which companies operate.

Management courses also seek to introduce techniques aimed at developing analytical, planning, creative, decision-making, problem-solving and communication skills. These techniques include case studies and role-playing exercises, and as far as possible these seek to simulate the kinds of situations that arise in the actual working environment. Management training institutions are increasingly establishing direct and close links with employers, and are involving them in decisions about the structure and content of courses and the training techniques used. This is reflected in the trend towards part-time and sandwich courses and the number of intensive post-experience courses for mature managers. This means that people are able to relate their knowledge and newly acquired management skills to the real-life situations they confront in their own companies. Those institutions providing courses can also make them more relevant to a specific industry or company, if that company indicates the particular requirements of its management development programme. Closer links with employers have also led to the practice of using people on management courses to tackle real-life problems arising within their own companies. This has the advantage of providing real-life solutions, which can be assessed subsequently in the work place, using the management techniques and skills learned.

Internal management development programmes

Despite the greater number and range of management courses, many large companies still rely to a large extent upon internal methods. Mergers and takeovers mean that companies are getting larger and their size can justify the employment of specialist training staff and the use of management development consultants.

ICL has invested £20 million in its own training facilities, which provide a range of courses covering information technology, management and personal skills. At Windsor in Berkshire, ICL has its own very extensive accommodation and leisure facilities for residential courses. There are over 200 specialist training staff and where a number of staff need training at the same time then they will also provide training at other convenient locations/centres. Such are the resources and success of this aspect of ICL's operations that it has been established as a subsidiary company known as Peritas, which also sells training courses to other companies.

Internal programmes allow the participants to become more familiar with the various features of their own company, such as its structure and systems, while also gaining experience in a wide range of real-life business activities where management skills can be applied. Any knowledge requirements may involve the use of external courses while a combination of the following methods may be used to develop management skills.

Job rotation

This involves moving people to new jobs, which may also be in different sections or departments and may generally carry the same level of authority and responsibility. This will help the individual to gain the experience that may be needed before they can be promoted. They will increase their understanding of what is involved in various jobs while also appreciating more fully how these jobs contribute to the company's objectives. As an international company, ICL regards exchanges on an international or cross-divisional basis as being particularly valuable for providing specific experience for high-potential employees in the early part of their career or for specialists who need to broaden their perspective and experience. The company also

ensures that during their initial period of employment young entrants have the opportunity to work in other functions, locations and units.

For example, ICL's World Wide Spares Division (Stevenage, Hertfordshire) has devised a four-year Commercial Traineeship Scheme designed for 18-year-old school/college leavers that combines placements with formal qualifications. Years one to three involve a series of six-month placements in sections dealing with customer support, warehouse and distribution, finance, materials, sales and marketing, and purchasing. The manager in each placement unit is then responsible for all aspects of the trainee's off-the-job training. In year four they specialize in a particular function such as finance. In the first two years they also study for the award of the BTEC Higher National Certificate in Business and Finance. A novel feature of this course is that the North Hertfordshire College delivers the course on ICL's training premises, and the pattern of attendance allows a three-year course to be concentrated into two years. In the following two years the trainees then follow a specialist course such as the Institute of Purchasing and Supply or the Diploma in Marketing.

Projects

A manager may be given a special assignment that involves tackling a problem that has arisen within the company and that will take them beyond the scope of their existing job. The manager will investigate the causes, nature and effects of the problem and put forward recommendations for dealing with it. An assignment could also be based upon an investigation into the issues surrounding the introduction of changes in such areas as production methods, technology, management techniques, the organizational structure or administrative system. Projects as part of training and development in ICL therefore have clear objectives and are selected on the basis of meeting the real needs of the individual and the company and are not just exercises for their own sake.

This project or assignment approach can also involve a group of junior managers who are brought together to form a board to handle such matters or to investigate ways of improving efficiency in their own departments.

When employees are brought together in this way they will learn to appreciate more fully what is involved in other people's

Large companies can offer development programmes on their own premises.

jobs and the factors that influence their respective views on the issues being dealt with. Whether they are acting as individuals or as a group, they may be given the authority to put their recommendations into practice. This kind of supervisory or management development will introduce the element of reality into their decision-making as they will be responsible for the results of the action to be taken.

Action learning

This technique is based upon the view that the skills of senior managers are best sharpened and enhanced if they face new challenges or problems. Managers are said to benefit from taking over new jobs in the same company or being seconded, for perhaps up to a year, to another company, where they will face different circumstances or problems. Action learning reflects the view that although knowledge, theory and simulated exercises can be of use in some areas of management development, there is no real substitute for the experience and learning gained from actually doing the job.

To some extent this technique also reflects the view that some people are naturally gifted and already possess the abilities needed to become a good manager, but their full potential will be exploited only if they are continually stretched by a realistic and challenging environment. This will make a greater demand upon them as managers, and as a result their existing skills will be improved upon and latent skills stimulated.

The role played by action learning is also recognized by business schools and business centres whose programmes may provide opportunities for managers to discuss action they have taken at work in regular group meetings. A group may comprise managers from different companies and areas of responsibility, so that there is an exchange of views and a discussion of any alternative action that could have been taken.

Coaching

This involves regular informal meetings between a manager and a subordinate to discuss the latter's performance in relation to the achievement of any objectives or targets. These sessions will help managers to identify an individual's strengths and weaknesses, but they must not come to be seen by subordinates solely as a way of bringing them to task for mistakes or a lack of progress.

Subordinates should be encouraged to discuss any current problems and to explain the reasoning behind any solutions that they propose to use. Managers can then offer advice and comment while subordinates analyse further the proposed course of action in terms of how the solution is to be implemented and likely effects upon various activities. These meetings can also be used to consider ways of improving performance in the area of work for which a subordinate is responsible. They may also be used to assess potential for promotion, by seeing how a subordinate has handled any extra authority or responsibility that has been assigned for the purposes of a particular project.

These coaching or counselling sessions should be properly structured and regarded by both parties as part of a continuing development programme. Subordinates should be encouraged to express their views on issues that effect their future with the company and their career ambitions.

The success of coaching depends heavily upon the skills of managers, and they in turn should be encouraged to acquire and develop coaching and counselling skills. Without such training, managers may not be aware that they are simply giving instructions and making decisions on behalf of subordinates without adequate explanation. This will adversely affect the confidence and motivation of employees.

ICL's 'Investing in People' programme identifies managers, with their expertise and experience, as making one of the most important contribution to the development of their staff by taking a more active and positive lead in the coaching process:

> In our industry in particular, managers must understand that profits are made by people, not by products. Consequently they must effectively manage, invest in and develop their people if they and ICL are to enjoy long term success
>
> 'The ICL Way' (a guide to ICL)

ICL managers therefore use the following techniques when coaching their staff:

- rehearsing them through an important presentation and giving feedback during and after the presentation;
- identifying and encouraging them to take on a new task which extends their job scope and provides experience in a new area;
- discussing the qualities of a role model and getting them to identify the reasons for that person's success;
- allowing them to go through a manager's in-tray and asking them to suggest how they might deal with each item;
- discussing how the working environment can affect job performance and the factors that influence such an environment;
- encouraging them to seek information relevant to their job and working environment by reading books, newspapers, magazines and internal publications;
- delegating more responsibilities.

Open learning

Within ICL, use is made of open/distance learning programmes such as those supplied by the Henley Management Centre. For example, some ICL staff work towards the Certificate in Supervisory Management by completing a series of course modules mainly on a home-study basis over a period of between ten and fifteen months. The Centre supplies the employee with workbooks, videos, audio tapes and computer software, while ICL ensures that additional support on developing skills and work-placed assignments and activities is provided by assigning individuals to suitable managers. Workshops are also held at the Henley Centre and this element will also bring greater interaction between employees from different companies.

'Quality the ICL Way'

In 1986, ICL committed £2.5 million to the launch of a company-wide quality improvement process. The company recognized that it was part of an industry where product differentiation was rapidly decreasing because of the widespread availability of advances in technology. ICL therefore aimed to gain a competitive advantage by achieving a reputation as a company with the highest quality ranking. The resulting quality improvement process was based upon a common definition of quality, and this was 'conformance to requirements'. It was also based upon a shared understanding that these requirements are determined by the customer and this would be the case whether the 'customer' was a client or a colleague.

This programme, under the banner of 'Quality the ICL Way', was not limited to the manufacturing operations but was implemented in all areas of the company. About half a million worker-hours were dedicated to educating and training a workforce spread over seventy countries in the skills of quality improvement, and to putting them in practice. Over the first three years of the quality improvement programme, ICL made dramatic progress in many areas, achieving, for example, faster delivery times, greater product reliability, higher output per employee, a lower percentage of unresolved software bugs, a reduction in the level of inventories and a stronger image in the market-place.

Higher quality and better customer care were the objectives behind ICL's 'Quality the ICL Way' programme. Independent research had suggested the company needed to improve customer satisfaction. About 10,000 staff, 3,500 managers, 250 quality professionals and 100 facilitators took part in the programme.

A subsequent survey showed ICL had improved its satisfaction rating by 63 per cent. Corporate results for 1991 showed increases in revenue, market share and productivity.

The Times, 4 February 1993

In 1991, ICL introduced the second phase of its quality improvement process, and this gave customers even more attention. Known as 'Customer Care the ICL Way', this involved using the quality techniques that had been developed earlier to meet and then go beyond the requirements of customers, exceeding their expectations. Thus 'conformance to requirements' as a definition of customer care was no longer enough. The decision to focus upon customers was taken for several reasons.

- The average person who experiences bad service tells nine others about it, and 13 per cent tell more than twenty others. In comparison, people who receive excellent service only tell three or four others about it.
- It can cost around five times as much to acquire new custom as it does to retain existing custom.
- Increasing customer-retention by just 5 per cent can raise profits by 25 to 85 per cent.
- Technical differences between rival products are getting smaller, so quality and customer care will be key factors that differentiate products.
- The company was seen in some markets as being less caring than its competitors.

This Customer Care involved three major commitments:

1 the company would be easier to deal with;
2 it would stay close to its customers;
3 it would keep its promises.

All employees had to make a personal commitment to put the customer before their own or organizational requirements. To measuring performance in relation to Customer Care, it would be necessary to consider not how the company sees that performance but how the customers describe it. Thus, in a comprehensive survey, ICL asks customers what they feel about products, service and employees.

ICL also wanted its employees to adopt a certain attitude and therefore achieve a certain standard when doing business. It wanted them to aim to make the company the first-choice supplier, and to avoid the 'we can't win them all' approach. The company's objective was for ICL to be a household name for quality and customer care by 1994.

Four principles of customer care

DEFINITION
Exceeding customer expectations
not merely meeting them

SYSTEM
Personal service
not just following the process

STANDARD
First choice supplier
not we can't win them all

MEASURE
What the customer says it is
not what we think

By 1992 every manager had completed an intensive workshop as the beginning of a company-wide education process, and this ensured a common and thorough understanding of Customer Care. These sessions also required managers to identify those aspects of their own projects where the main principles of Customer Care could be applied.

Customer Care and communication skills

ICL paid a great deal of attention to improving its employees' communications skills because of their obvious importance when dealing with customers. The following is based upon extracts from a document used to develop communication skills within ICL.

Communicating with people
Communication is the successful passing of a message (information) from one person to another. There must be feedback from the sender to ensure that the message has been received and understood.

Sending a message
- Check that there is a need to communicate – sort out the objectives.
- Consider the attitudes and knowledge of the receivers, e.g. are they technically minded?
- Decide how the message is to be sent, e.g. written, face to face, phone, pictorial.
- Put the message into an overall content.
- Select the appropriate structure, content and language.
- Small pieces of information are easier to digest than long, complicated messages.
- In sending a message encourage and respond to feedback.

Questioning to obtain information/feedback

- Background information is needed to give the overall picture and this involves open questions, which allow a wide range of answers. They usually start with how, why, or what, e.g. 'How will the operators be trained?'
- Diagnostic information is required when referring to a specific situation and is obtained using closed questions. These have a specific answer and it is often 'yes' or 'no', e.g. 'Will your engineers carry out the training?'
- When speaking and seeking feedback to check understanding, use an indirect and more subtle technique such as 'So how will this effect you ...?' rather than 'You know what will happen then don't you.'
- Ask only one question at a time and wait for an answer.

Barriers to listening

- Our thought processes operate four times faster than most people speak and as a listener we may become bored and our mind is likely to wander.
- We may regard what is being said as dull, out of date or irrelevant and close our mind to it and therefore miss the vital pieces of information.
- We all have our prejudices and fixed ideas and a customer may say something with which we disagree. We may react by pretending to listen and restraining our thoughts rather than risk an argument. No attempt is made therefore to discover the reasons for their comments.
- The customer makes comments that are too complex or technical for us to understand and we cannot make the effort to follow or we are too embarrassed to ask questions. We remain silent with a glazed look until the conversation comes back to our level, but then show our earlier lack of understanding by an inappropriate comment.
- The customer gives a great number of facts and we try to absorb and understand him or her, or we lose track of what is being said. We must therefore learn to focus on the key facts or slow the customer down with pointed questions and note taking.
- Persistent reference to such issues as budget problems, policy decisions, competitors, and spares problems may raise our emotions and distract us. We must learn to remain cool and unruffled when we hear them.

Listening with empathy

- Listen in an understanding way and make sure that you are aware of any emotional aspect revealed through tone of voice or choice of language.
- Do not interrupt unless asking for clarification.
- Listen for feeling as well as meaning. Most messages have two elements: content and feeling. For example, is the speaker critical, neutral, using their own or somebody else's idea, optimistic or pessimistic or being held responsible for any problems they are describing?
- If face to face then listen with your whole self: maintain eye contact, lean forward and avoid forming barriers with your arms.

- Listen for the theme of the message and do not be distracted by side issues or incidental remarks.
- Focus on the customer's needs and select the facts that relate to those needs.
- Be alert for omissions because the essential message may actually be indicated by what is not said.
- Look for the 'why' behind each statement and make this the basis for your own questions. This technique will also help the speaker to identify and then associate the causes with the problems.
- Ask questions when you do not fully understand what the customer is saying.
- Make selective notes.

Aids to listening

- Seek clarification to make sure you heard and understood correctly. This also helps the speaker to develop their thinking. This can involve saying 'So the situation is ...' or 'Do you mean ...?'
- Engage in reflection that is rephrasing what the speaker says. This is important because it indicates understanding without suggesting that you either agree or disagree with the speaker. Reflection also encourages further relevant information and shows you are interested and alert.
- Certain kinds of neutral expressions can also show you are still switched on and encourage the customer to continue. These include 'I see', 'That's interesting', 'I understand', and 'Really?'
- Summarizing can bring into focus what has been said and can also encourage more thoughts. Such a technique may be introduced using 'Well, so far it appears that ...', 'So the situation as you see it is ...', 'If I understand you correctly, the situation is as follows ...'.

The features of a good listener

Listening is an art requiring skill, discipline and practice. A good listener must control his or her ego, intellect, emotions and behaviour and pay complete attention to the speaker. At the same time a good listener will keep an open mind and show a genuine interest in the speaker and his or her views.

We lose the benefit of body language when we talk on the telephone, both in using it ourselves and observing it in others.

Activities

Short answer questions

1 What are the costs to a company of failing to train and develop its workforce?
2 Why will training allow a company to sustain its current level of output with a smaller workforce?
3 Explain how training and development programmes can help to reduce labour turnover and absenteeism.
4 Give examples of advances in technology that have required user industries to train its employees in new skills.
5 What factors are likely to encourage an employee to take full advantage of a training programme?
6 What are the advantages of on-the-job training and why is it particularly suitable for manual skills?
7 What are the advantages of off-the-job training being supported by a period of on-the-job training?
8 List some of the social and personal skills that you think will help to make a good manager.
9 How can companies use real business situations to develop management skills?
10 What kinds of problems can arise if supervisors and managers have no formal training to help deliver on-the-job training and development programmes?

Local investigation

Each student should identify local institutions that offer courses to support the training and development programmes provided by companies and other employers in their area.

Tasks

1 Having surveyed the courses described in their publicity material, select an appropriate part-time or evening course that will meet the needs of the following:
   (a) companies employing people who need to acquire basic computer skills;
   (b) people who manage surgeries on behalf of doctors;
   (c) a company wishing to prepare an employee with a BTEC HNC in Business Studies for promotion to a higher management post in its central purchasing department;
   (d) trainee care assistants at residential homes for the elderly;
   (e) companies wanting a two-year course for electronics engineers coming from school with good GCSE results;
   (f) people being trained to a high level in the software engineering aspects of computing;
   (g) graduates with degrees in Business Studies, including an option in Marketing, whose employers want them to obtain a specialist Marketing qualification;
   (h) employees currently holding senior supervisory positions;
   (i) a health farm recruiting young people who will be trained in a range of health and beauty treatments;
   (j) catering establishments wishing to meet the training aspects of the Food Hygiene Act.

Local colleges provide a wide range of courses to meet the off-the-job training and development needs of local employers.

2 Having identified appropriate courses, obtain the relevant leaflets and give a brief outline of the knowledge and/or skills that each of them seeks to develop.
3 List the specialist short courses offered to develop the knowledge and skills of those in management positions.

Role play

This role-play exercise should be conducted after having established the importance of the oral communication skills outlined on pages 47–8, which featured in 'Customer Care the ICL Way'. It will help you to recognize the importance of oral communication skills for people in sales or after-sales services when dealing with customers. You will also appreciate the importance of self-development in relation to personal and social skills when handling a face-to-face business situation.

Tasks

1 Select a product of some kind that is interesting in terms of features such as design materials, ingredients, performance, technology, after sales service, methods of payment, special offers or other factors that are likely to be significant selling points. Such products may include a camera, personal stereo, hairdryer, hand-held computer

game, shaver, calculator, trainers, sports equipment, crash helmet, car/motorcycle/bicycle accessories, luggage, toiletry and cosmetics, magazine, or any other item that is easy to carry.

2   Find out as much as you can about your product from labels, instruction leaflets, manuals and sales brochures and draw up a list of selling points and answers to the questions you would expect from potential customers.

3   Each student should then assume the role of a salesperson and give a brief talk about their product and why it is good value at its current price. During this session the salesperson should question his or her 'customers' to gauge their opinions, identify their needs and determine the reasons why they may have recently bought a competing product. The salesperson must also expect to be questioned by the customers and listen to their opinions of his or her product.

4   When acting as a potential customer each student should score each salesperson on the form below:

General presentation of information						
(attracting and sustaining interest)	1	2	3	4	5	6
Choice of language	1	2	3	4	5	6
Tone of voice	1	2	3	4	5	6
Clarity of speech	1	2	3	4	5	6
Stimulating feedback/participation	1	2	3	4	5	6
Asking questions	1	2	3	4	5	6
Listening to customers	1	2	3	4	5	6
Answering questions	1	2	3	4	5	6
Eye contact	1	2	3	4	5	6
Product knowledge	1	2	3	4	5	6
Personality and manner	1	2	3	4	5	6
Dress and general appearance	1	2	3	4	5	6
Posture and general bearing	1	2	3	4	5	6

Marking scheme: 1 Very poor;   2 Poor;
3 Satisfactory;   4 Good;
5 Very good;   6 Excellent.

5   The marks awarded by customers for each salesperson should be averaged to determine the salesperson with the most effective communications and social and personal skills/qualities.

Data Analysis

The following questions are based upon the data in the table on pages 41 and 42

1   Give possible reasons why the percentage of managers, administrators and professionals who undertook training that leads to a qualification/credit is much smaller than other groups ('personal' includes health care and 'protective' includes police).

2   Why do you think that the percentage of job-related training was highest in the professional occupations? Why is it lowest amongst sales, plant and machine operatives?

3   What factors could explain why a higher percentage of women received training in certain occupations and why it was lower in others, such as 'craft and related'.

4   Why does the percentage of people receiving an element of off-the-job training differ between occupations?

Introduction

Toyota manufactures vehicles and parts at some twenty-nine plants in twenty-two countries employing more than 100,000 people worldwide. The Toyota vehicles on sale in the UK are the Starlet, Corolla, Carina E, Camry, MR2, Celica, Supra, Previa, Landcruiser ll and VX and the Lexus. Commercial vehicles on the UK market are the Liteace, Hilux and Hiace and the Optimo which is an eighteen-to-twenty-one seat luxury passenger coach. In 1991 the company produced 4.75 million vehicles – the third largest number after General Motors and Ford. Toyota exported 1.7 million vehicles in 1991 compared with about 1 million by Nissan and about 800,000 by Mazda.

Growth and development

The origins of Toyota can be traced back to Sakichi Toyoda, who was the inventor of Japan's first automatic loom. In 1910 he travelled to the USA where he was particularly impressed by the motorcar, but on returning he still concentrated on the main business of developing looms. This resulted in the establishment of the Toyoda Spinning and Weaving Co. Ltd in 1918 and the Toyoda Automatic Loom Works Ltd in 1926.

In 1929, Britain's Platt Brothers, the largest manufacturer of textile machinery in the world, bought the production and sales rights to one of Toyoda's automatic looms for £100,000. Sakichi Toyoda gave this money to his son, Kiichiro Toyoda, to fund the development of motor vehicle technology. Thus the initial funding for Toyota actually came from Britain. After the death of his father in 1930, Kiichiro took over the business. Following a visit to the USA he decided to carry out research into building a small petrol engine.

In the early 1930s Japan's motor vehicle market was dominated by imports from the USA, but in 1933 Kiichiro Toyoda set up a Motor Vehicle Department to produce cars. By 1935 the first prototype was completed and in the following year the first model was launched. In 1937 the Toyota Motor Company was founded and its Koromo Plant began production in 1938.

After the Second World War, the Japanese economy was left in ruins and total industrial production was only one-tenth of its pre-war levels. When Toyota restarted its car production, it had to do so with run-down and outdated plant and machinery. In 1947 Toyota produced its first small car, but in 1950 there was a long and bitter strike. This has proved to be the only strike in Toyota's history because, after the eventual return to work, labour and management became firmly convinced of the importance of mutual trust and cooperation.

Production systems were improved in the late 1950s and early 1960s, and in 1959 Toyota's Motomachi Plant became the country's first car plant used exclusively for passenger car production. The rapid growth in production from this period onwards can be seen in the first of the two graphs below At the same time Toyota greatly improved its export performance as shown in the second graph.

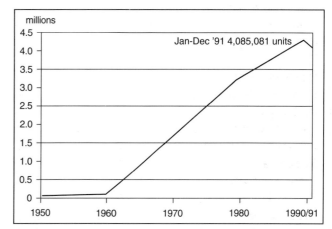

Total domestic unit production.

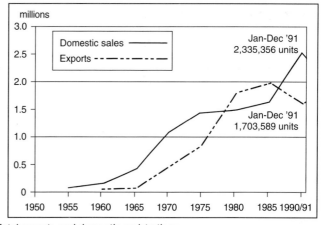

Total exports and domestic registrations.

During the late 1980s Toyota began to establish manufacturing operations in some of its key markets. Output from those overseas plants would have partly replaced exports to those markets from its plants in Japan.

In 1965 Toyota developed models that appealed to the Americans at a time when the market had already shown an interest in 'compact' cars such as the Volkswagen Beetle. In the early 1970s the Organization of Petroleum Exporting Countries (OPEC) also engineered a fivefold increase in the world price of oil and that, coupled with political instability in the Middle East, threatened to produce an oil shortage. Many American buyers were attracted by the small-engined and hence fuel-efficient Japanese models, and the USA soon became Toyota's major export market. Sales to the USA continued to increase in the late 1970s, but Toyota's penetration of the American market caused the US government to 'require' that Toyota and other Japanese manufacturers should voluntarily restrain their exports to the country. In 1984, production started on a joint venture with General Motors in California, but by 1986 Toyota had established its first wholly owned production plant at Georgetown, Kentucky. Two years later its first US-built Toyota was driven off the production line, and in 1993 over 470,000 Toyota vehicles were built in the USA. Toyota sales in the USA grew from 11,072 in 1965 to over 1 million in 1993. Its vehicles are now sold in more than 160 countries and in 1993 Toyota had 163 importers and distributors who in turn supplied over 7,300 dealerships.

Toyota made its first exports to Europe in 1962, and between then and 1993 it signed distribution agreements in twenty-three countries where there are now around 3,400 Toyota dealers. The Toyota Technical Centre of Europe was established outside Brussels in 1987 and in 1989 the Toyota Design Centre of Europe was set up on the same site. This Design Centre plays an important part in the design of cars for the European market. The company's first production activity in Europe began in 1968 when a local company in Portugal produced commercial vehicles under licence at a rate of 12,000 per year. Since 1987 a French company has carried out the production of forklifts with Toyota's technical assistance and produces approximately 2,000 forklifts a year. A major involvement came in 1989 when Toyota and Volkswagen AG started the joint production of pick-up trucks in Hanover, Germany. This joint project produces approximately 12,000 trucks a year. In 1989 Toyota announced plans to build its first manufacturing plants for the European market in the UK. Burnaston in Derbyshire was chosen for a vehicle manufacturing plant and Deeside in North Wales for an engine plant (see page 61).

Europe is now the largest single market in the world and, before the deepening recession of the early 1990s, car sales reached 13.53 million in 1991. By the year 2000 Toyota estimates that the European market, including Russia and Eastern Europe, will become a 20 million vehicle market.

Vehicle manufacturing plant in Burnaston, Derbyshire.

The general role of production and the efficient management of physical resources

Production covers all those activities that commence with the receipt of raw materials and eventually give rise to an end product. This product may take the form of a component that is then passed on to another company, or one that is ready for final use, such as an item of machinery or a consumer durable. Production management will deal mainly with the planning and control of all the various stages of production in order to make the most efficient use of a company's resources.

The kind of production processes carried out within any particular organization will vary according to the size of the company, the initial state of raw materials and components, the extent to which they must be worked upon and the size of the production run needed to meet the demand for the company's product or products. How the production is organized and which areas tend to command the greatest attention will differ widely even between companies in the same industry. A manufacturer producing cars for a mass market, for example, will use production methods that differ in various ways from those adopted by a company producing custom-built vehicles. Similarly, different industries lend themselves to the application of different kinds of technologies. Whatever the size and nature of a firm's output, however, it must organize and manage its production as efficiently as possible, since a failure to do so will mean higher unit costs, a loss of price competitiveness, lost market share, and falling profits.

Whatever the nature of the undertaking, the aims of production planning and control will be to decide upon the physical means by which the product is to be achieved in terms of plant, machinery and equipment, and where production should be located. It will also cover the scheduling for the various stages and the personnel to be involved in such stages. The production plan will then seek to ensure that once the programme is established it is followed, and that any changes in the programme at a later date are also followed with equal attention. The main aspects of production control that concern those working in the department are:

1　involvement in product development;
2　determining levels and types of product;
3　design of premises;
4　organization of manufacturing;
5　scheduling;
6　materials control;
7　stock control;
8　maintenance;
9　handling systems;
10　quality control;
11　work study.

Involvement in product development

The production department will maintain close contact with the research and development department. In particular, it will need to be closely involved in the design stages of a new product. This is so that it can gain an early indication of the extent to which existing production techniques can cope with the processes involved, and thus assess the areas where changes might have to be made either in the design of the product itself or in the company's production facilities. The product must be designed to meet the customers' needs, but must be able to be produced efficiently and profitably.

Detailed drawings and specifications will be used so that the intended product can be reproduced as exactly as possible. Computer-aided design techniques are increasingly applied for this purpose. The specifications will include descriptions and directions relating to the various processes involved, together with a parts list which will have its own drawings and specifications. The specifications will also designate the tolerances needed and at the same time remain within limits that both machines and operatives can readily accommodate.

Cost control will be introduced at the early stages, to assess the implications of the number and range of operations, the materials and the assembly work involved. Efforts will be made to achieve further standardization, by exploring, for example, the extent to which parts and components can be drawn from or used in other products already in production. The design may then be simplified to keep it within a certain range of separate components or operations, and decisions will be made on standard sizes, capacities or other features of the product. These areas are investigated in order to gain the advantages associated with long production runs.

When the design has been fully developed, prototypes can be produced for experimental and test purposes. These may be followed by a larger pre-production run to assess the performance of the production facilities and, depending upon the results, alterations may be made to certain aspects of the production plan, such as those concerned with equipment, tools, factory layout and communications systems between different sections.

Determining levels and types of product

A dominant factor in determining the way in which production is organized is the number of individual products or different levels of standardized products that are required. This will determine the kinds of manual skills needed, the capacity and capability of machines, and the factory layout itself, including intermediate handling and final storage. At one extreme there is job or unit production where the product is specifically designed and produced to meet the requirements of a particular customer. An example of this would be the design, manufacture and installation of a sophisticated piece of high-technology machinery to meet the specialist needs of another company. Unit production requires that labour, machinery, equipment and factory layout are of a highly flexible nature to deal with individual orders for custom-built products.

Longer production runs are usually associated with batch production. This is a repetitive, though not necessarily continuous, form of output. The size of a batch will depend upon what amounts to an economic quantity in the light of the changes that need to be made to tools, equipment and machinery before moving over to another batch. Sometimes companies that need to even out the workload between various sections of the production department, or the company as a whole, will find it useful to organize production so that it handles a variety of processes. Batch production is likely to take place in such areas as footwear, clothing, furniture, textiles, steel, paint, food and publishing, where product ranges are manufactured.

Mass- or line-production is used where there is a large demand for a product and a flow of output can be maintained.

The Lexus LS400 took six years to develop, and involved 2,300 technicians, 1,400 engineers, 450 prototypes and 2.7 million test miles.

Robots at work on a Toyota production line.

Alternative versions of the product may be offered, but these would not involve any significant variation from the standard. This type of production will involve more specific and longer-term arrangements regarding skills, machinery and equipment, layout and communications. Investment in this kind of single-purpose capacity will involve very large sums of money, and the work of the sales forecasting unit will be vital in ensuring that optimum use can be made of capacity. This is because its specific and inflexible nature may not readily lend itself to alternative uses if the market does not live up to expectations. Mass-production techniques are found in companies producing motor vehicles, domestic appliances such as washing machines, and home entertainment products such as video cassette recorders and televisions. These have mass markets and because their production can be broken down into a series of relatively straightforward processes and operations they can be mass-produced on assembly lines.

Design of premises

Production planning will assess the extent to which the existing design of premises and their specific site and general location will allow production to be carried out efficiently and profitably. The choice of location will be affected by such factors as the size and skills of the labour force required, the supply of raw materials, components and other inputs, transport links and the location of the market. The production department will then consider the design of the premises. Mass-production will generally involve an extensive single-storey facility while other types of production may allow a multi-storey building. The production department will seek a building design that meets various requirements: for example, allowing the most efficient use to be made of the technology available, siting certain activities in close proximity to each other, enabling the internal movement of materials, components and personnel, and providing the conditions for a healthy and safe working environment.

Organization of manufacturing

Production planning will be undertaken to organize the product through its various manufacturing stages. This may start with the initial treatment of raw materials, the manufacture of components, sub-assembly and final assembly. The whole of this exercise must be carefully planned so that all sections are operating at optimum levels and the various operations are coordinated to avoid both bottle-necks and idle capacity.

The production planning department will liaise with the marketing department to transform the latter's requirements into detailed instructions for the sections involved in production so that the overall manufacturing process is smooth and efficient. Production programmes or schedules will be produced to deal with the timetabling of the processes and the quantities involved to achieve suitable targets.

Having formulated schedules, works orders will be issued to authorize production to meet orders. A works order will contain details such as the code and job numbers allocated to it, the description of the product, the quantity, the materials required, the operations to be performed upon the product, the sequence of operations, and the time allowed for each operation.

Scheduling

A section will be allocated the task of keeping schedules up to date and tracing the progress of works orders. This will help to ensure that production sections are meeting their targets and keeping to timetables. Information from this progress control will allow the actual progress to be compared with the planned timetable. Differences can then be investigated to stop any shortcomings becoming more serious departures from the production schedule.

Materials control

Another aspect of production control is materials control. This contributes to efficient production by ensuring that materials are provided in the correct quality and quantity, in the right place and at the appropriate time. The materials control section keeps in close contact with the other departments involved in such work as the purchase of materials and other items, their receipt, storage and allocation from stores.

Stock control

Effective production control requires details of the current stock position in the stores so that production is not held up by shortages. Stock control must seek to strike a balance between ensuring that sufficient stocks of various items are held to allow production to proceed smoothly and ensuring against too much capital being tied up in stocks. Other factors to be considered concerning stocks include the availability of storage space, likely price fluctuations, perishability or possible obsolescence. The time-lags between ordering and delivery and the quantities of stocks that make up the most economic orders are also important factors. This control will be exerted not only over the direct stores used for materials, components and finished parts, but also over indirect stores for the tools used in manual or machine operations.

Maintenance

Adequate maintenance of plant, equipment, machinery and premises will be vital, since breakdowns or inefficient operation will lead to a loss of valuable output. Large capital-intensive industries, in particular, incur very large fixed costs, and capacity must be used fully to spread overhead costs over as large a level of output as possible. A breakdown in a single operation can lead to a complete halt in production. Stoppages may also be caused by a failure to meet the requirements of the Factories Act and the Health and Safety Act.

A great deal of the maintenance designed to prevent breakdowns will be aimed at replacement schemes which may involve the replacement of sound parts. Much of this is calculated upon the basis of probability and the expected life of the components that make up the plant, machinery and equipment.

Handling systems

Production must be supported by an efficient handling system. This must deal with the initial receipt of raw materials and components, their processing and assembly, finishing, packaging and eventual dispatch or storage. Items must move smoothly between operations so that neither labour or machinery is left idle. In many industries the system must handle items that are processed or operated upon while they are actually moving. Handling costs can be as much as 85 per cent in some industries, and increased efficiency in this area can have a marked effect upon competitiveness.

Quality control

The production department will be very concerned about maintaining certain quality standards. A standard for quality will be established and a control system introduced to ensure that it is maintained. Quality control may start with incoming materials and components and then operate at all stages of production. It can be very expensive to rectify faults or defects, particularly if they have gone unnoticed in a large quantity and items have to be scrapped. If they have already reached customers, then the producer's reputation and hence future sales can be seriously affected. Quality will be checked by inspection teams who will also be responsible for periodically checking the tools used in machinery to ensure that they still perform to their specification. This work will also cover the equipment used by the worker to check that the operation or process has been carried out within the agreed tolerances.

On the assembly line, workers have easy access to important information, as every vehicle carries sheets displaying relevant details of the vehicle's specifications.

Work study

Work study is used to improve methods and make a more efficient use of labour, materials and machine capacity. As production proceeds, lessons will be learned and faults corrected. A more positive approach can be taken by setting up a work study section to investigate possible areas for improvement. Work study will also ascertain the 'time allowed' for individual tasks and this provides important information for costing and planning and for creating the bonus schemes for operatives whereby in addition to a basic hourly rate they are paid extra for those tasks completed in the time allowed. By completing a job in less than the time allowed, operatives can use the time saved to pass on to more jobs that carry a bonus payment. Since the weekly bonus payment may be a significant part of their total earnings, this is an incentive to use all their time as productively as possible.

The Toyota approach to production and the efficient management of physical resources

When Toyota started to make cars in the 1930s, it was faced with a very small domestic market dominated by imported cars. Toyota recognized that its likely sales would not allow it to reap the kinds of economies of scale usually associated with a mass

assembly line. However, no motor vehicle manufacturer could expect to be competitive unless it operated the conveyor-based assembly line method of production introduced by Henry Ford. The company therefore had to find other ways of achieving the kinds of savings needed to make its assembly line method more efficient. These were the initial pressures that led to the essential features of a production method that, from the early 1970s in particular, became known throughout the world as the Toyota Production System. The system aims to shorten the time taken to convert customer orders into vehicle deliveries and is achieved by arranging the entire sequence from order to delivery in a single continuous flow. The company has consistently sought to find ways of shortening this sequence and making the flow even smoother. This is reflected in improvements in productivity and the quality of its products. In addition, Toyota needs to offer an increasing number of model variations to keep up with changing customer demand. In producing cars for the Japanese market for example, Toyota plants generally manufacture vehicles to some 45,000 different combinations of specifications such as body colour, engine size, type of gear box, and braking system. Assembly line techniques have therefore had to be adapted to cope with this greater diversification of output.

Just-in-time

When Kiichiro Toyoda set up his car manufacturing operation in the 1930s, he had to adapt the Henry Ford conveyor system to the small Japanese market. Mass-production required that each step in the production sequence was kept supplied with a variety of parts, as an entire line would grind to a halt if employees ran out of parts at any stage. To prevent shortages, car producers kept large stocks along their production lines. Given the size of the Japanese market, Toyota could not operate on this basis. Holding large stocks of parts would not only tie up scarce capital but would also prove costly in terms of storage space and the labour needed to handle the accumulated parts.

In response to this problem, Kiichiro developed a system in which the different processes in the assembly sequence were supplied only with the kinds and quantities of items that they needed and only when they needed them – in other words, 'just in time' for each sequence to be implemented. This just-in-time or JIT production management prevents the accumulation of excessive parts beside the line while ensuring that the process is not held up because a part is lacking. With JIT production management, everything that takes place throughout the production sequence contributes to satisfying customer orders.

JIT also affects Toyota's suppliers, who are expected to deliver major components to the plant exactly when needed. This requires very tight management of the supply chain and the development of close working relations with suppliers, who are seen as partners in a mutually beneficial exercise. This working method leads to the company and its suppliers developing a deeper understanding of each other's needs. The result is a more stable relationship and more consistent quality.

Traditional mass production systems were 'push' systems, where each process in the various stages of production passed its output on to the next process, regardless of the latter's actual requirements. By contrast, the Toyota Production System is a 'pull' system whereby each process withdraws items from the preceding process only in the types and quantities needed and only at the time they are needed. The items used for one process in a plant therefore determine the production flow for earlier processes at the same plant. This also means that the items used at an assembly plant will determine the production flow at the plants where the parts are manufactured. Nobody produces or transports any items that are not necessary to the following process.

Kanban

For JIT production to function smoothly, all the processes throughout the production sequence must operate in conjunction with each other. It is the *kanban* system that helps to ensure that motor vehicle plants are kept supplied with the thousands of items they need on a just-in-time basis. A *kanban*, which means sign-board in Japanese, is usually a printed card in a clear plastic sleeve. A card accompanies each item or stock of items that moves through the production system. The information carried by all the cards in the system controls the flow of all the different parts to the various areas where they are needed.

An employee removes the *kanban* from the item, or from the first item in a stock, when it is used. The *kanban* is then returned to the preceding process to indicate the need to produce additional items. A similar system is used to send such information back to outside suppliers.

A worker inspects the kanban *on a box of parts. Information on the* kanban *includes the supplier name, the receiving area at Toyota, and the location in the plant where the item will be used.*

The *kanban* system means that Toyota's employees take responsibility for managing their own jobs. This is because when an employee removes *kanban* from components before mounting them on a vehicle, and sends them back to the preceding processes, he or she is actually shouldering an important part of managing the material flow, and this system plays an important role in the management function of ordering parts and stock control.

Total Quality Management

Since 'safety stocks' are no longer available to cover for materials shortages, all items are assumed to be usable. This means

that the JIT system cannot operate without a top management commitment to Total Quality Management (TQM). This ensures that every aspect of the company's operations, not just the production and assembly cycle, is managed in ways that guarantee good quality products. TQM must therefore be company-wide, involve both management and employees, and function as an approach based upon the *prevention* of errors and faults rather than the traditional policy of detection and correction. JIT means that TQM must also be adopted by suppliers, as there will not be any inspection of incoming components, and suppliers are expected to meet a 'zero defects' standard of quality. Although the essential features of TQM originated in the USA during the 1940s, they were mainly developed and applied by Toyota and other Japanese companies in the 1950s. It was only in the 1980s that TQM started to have an impact in the West. Companies started to reduce their dependence upon inspection to achieve high quality and instead build quality into all their activities and functions.

Customer satisfaction is at the heart of all Toyota's operations, whether research and development, design, manufacturing or retailing and servicing, and good quality is central to achieving customer satisfaction. Poor quality can give rise to a variety of costs, such as those associated with rejects and scrap, rectification, the need for an inspection department, the work carried out for customers under guarantees and the effects upon market share if quality is inconsistent. In some cases the defect may also lead to legal action, which has implications in terms of both financial cost and public opinion. TQM is therefore essential, not only for the operation of a JIT production system, but also for the competitive value of the end product.

Jidoka

Another feature of the Toyota Production System is *jidoka*. This is concerned with making machines respond 'intelligently' in the same way that a human would. It has its origins in the automatic looms invented by Sakichi Toyoda. A loom developed in 1902 would stop automatically if any of the threads snapped, just as a human worker would do. Since then, the principle of stopping work whenever a defect or abnormality is found has been fundamental to the Toyota Production System. Examples of *jidoka* equipment include fail-safe features that prevent employees from mounting or assembling equipment incorrectly and sensors that prevent machines from operating when a defect occurs. An advantage of *jidoka* is that it identifies a problem by stopping the machinery or equipment exactly where it is when the problem first occurs, thereby making it easier to determine the cause of the problem. Perhaps the most important advantage of this system is that, because machines stop automatically when abnormalities occur, there is no need to have operators watching over each machine continuously. This makes for very significant improvements in the productivity of labour.

Employees themselves are also able to stop the production flow if they identify or suspect a problem, by pulling an overhead cable or pushing a button. Both automatic and manual forms of *jidoka* prevent defective parts from reaching further stages of production and avoid the waste that would result from producing a series of defective items. *Jidoka* also helps avoid major mechanical breakdowns because machinery and equipment can be seriously damaged if they handle defective or incorrectly assembled items.

Pulling on the overhead cable or pushing the button lights up a number on a large display board called an *andon*, which tells

Sensors prevent a stamping press from operating when a body panel is not positioned properly on the lower member of a pair of stamping dies. These dies together weigh 22 tons, and would crack easily if the stamping press were to slam them together when the workpiece was missing or wrongly positioned.

The numbered lamps on the andon light up when automatic sensors in the equipment detect a problem.

the supervisor in which work station the problem has arisen. The line itself does not stop immediately, so if the supervisor is able to deal with the problem very quickly then he or she can pull the cable again to prevent the line from stopping. Most problems can be dealt with in a matter of seconds, but if it takes longer then the line will stop when it has reached the next 'fixed' position. All the jobs at the different work stations on the line are scheduled so that workers are between steps in their work at the same time. If the line has to be stopped, therefore, disruption to the rest of the line will be minimized if it keeps going until it reaches the 'fixed' position. This system avoids the errors and quality problems that could arise if workers are obliged to stop before they have completed the whole of a particular process. *Jidoka* therefore builds quality into the production processes and means that all workers are actively involved on a continuing basis with another management function – quality control assurance.

Kaizen

Kaizen means continuous improvement, and is a process designed to ensure maximum quality and reduce waste in all areas of Toyota's operations. Workers operate in teams of about eight, and team leaders are responsible for establishing the procedures and standards for their own team's work. Standardized work means that each worker will then follow certain guide-lines and in doing so will maintain targets in terms of productivity, quality and working conditions. *Kaizen* involves teams of

employees meeting regularly to revise their standardized work so that targets are continually being improved upon and costs reduced. Team members can generate ideas for revising work methods, reorganizing and redistributing work, rearranging layouts and changing automation, and supervisors will lead the implementation of these ideas.

The most common target for *kaizen* is waste, and this refers to everything that increases the costs of production without making a useful contribution to meeting customers' orders. *Kaizen* focuses especially on seven sources of waste:

1 over-production;
2 waiting imposed by an inefficient work sequence;
3 transport;
4 processing workpieces more than they require;
5 inventory in excess of immediate needs;
6 motion that does not contribute to work;
7 correction required because of defects.

Over-production

This is the worst kind of waste because it conflicts with JIT production. It will also make it difficult to recognize the need for improvement because both supervisors and workers who are busy on what amounts to over-production will not be aware that some of their labour is being wasted.

Waiting imposed by an inefficient work sequence

An inefficient work sequence can lead to employees waiting idle when they could be working. An example of this is shown in the diagram below. The process shown involved three semi-automatic machines with three operators carrying out separate

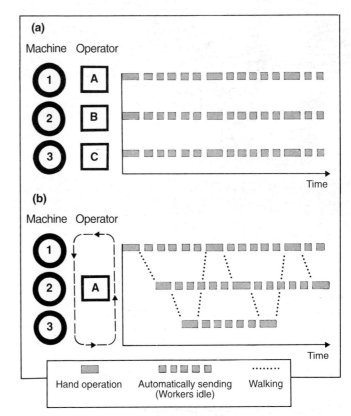

Improvement to eliminate unnecessary waiting: (a) the process before improvement; (b) the process after improvement.

operations. The employees would perform their work simultaneously and then wait in unison for the next item to arrive from the previous machine. The idle time was eliminated by reorganizing the work so that it could be carried out by a single worker who now moves from machine A to machine B and then on to machine C before returning to A.

Transport

Inefficient layouts result in moving parts and materials more than is necessary. Machines and production lines should be as close as possible and workpieces and materials should progress from one machine to the next without stopping at any temporary storage space.

Processing workpieces more than they require

Many items have to be precision-made and workers must work to very small tolerances. In some areas however, excessive processing would be wasteful. A milling machine operator for example is wasting any time that is spent achieving a tolerance of ± 0.001 mm when ± 0.01 mm is entirely adequate.

Inventory in excess of immediate needs

The prevention of excess inventory is fundamental to the Toyota Production System. Achieving a smooth flow of work throughout the system will prevent any process from making more of an item than the next process requires. If any unnecessary inventory does accumulate, it will become the focus of *kaizen* activities and will generally lead to measures that produce an even smoother flow of work.

Motion that does not contribute to work

Processes often involve more movement by people and by machines than is really necessary to complete the task at hand.

The illustration below shows an example of *kaizen* eliminating unnecessary movement. As a safety precaution, workbenches are often equipped with photosensors that prevent potentially dangerous equipment from starting until the operator has completely withdrawn his or her hands from over the workbench.

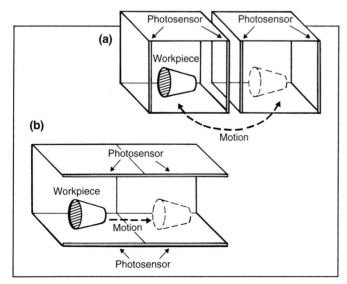

Improvement to eliminate unnecessary motion: (a) the process before improvement; (b) the process after improvement.

The first machine will operate as soon as the worker's hands are moved from under its particular sensors. Before the improvement, this could only be done by moving backwards from the machine; after the improvement the worker needed only to move his or her hands sideways from the first machine to the second.

Correction required because of defects

Standardized work and *jidoka* are designed to ensure that quality objectives are consistently met. By avoiding defects in the first place, wastage of materials, labour and other resources will be avoided.

Kaizen involves giving workers full responsibility for their jobs. Each worker is responsible for the quality and efficiency of his or her part of the production process and must deliver a quality product to the 'customer' (the next stage on the line). At the same time, workers will actively suggest *kaizen* ideas for improving quality, productivity and working conditions. Voluntary employee participation takes place in quality control circles and throughout the company-wide Creative Suggestion Scheme. In 1990 Toyota employees in Japan contributed about 2 million suggestions for improvements and 97 per cent of these were implemented.

In one plant in South Africa, for example, inspectors were used to check that all bolts had been tightened, but their role was virtually eliminated when the factory adopted a suggestion from an employee team. This involved using a dollop of paint in the torque wrench sockets so that when the operators tightened the bolts a trace of paint was left on the bolt heads, which made it immediately obvious if any bolts had not been sufficiently tightened. Teamwork is therefore an essential element of the Toyota Production System, and the company holds the view that a well-coordinated group can accomplish far more than the most gifted individual.

Heijunka

On the basis of a daily production plan, managers at Toyota plants decide on the exact sequence of items to produce at their plants in one day. This is called *heijunka* sequential planning and involves distributing the volume of output and model specifications evenly over the span of production. The output of Toyota plants will correspond to the diverse mix of model variations ordered by customers. To achieve this, the production of the different body types is staggered evenly over the course of the day, so that a variety of such body types moves along the same assembly line at the same time. It would be possible for production to be organized in such a way that the daily operating period was divided into several parts and each was then devoted exclusively to the production of a particular model. This system, however, would produce a level and pattern of output that differed from the continuing variety of model variations sold by Toyota dealers, and hence stocks of finished vehicles awaiting customers.

Concentrating production in this way would also produce peaks that would impose a disproportionate share of production on each team at a time in the preceding processes. Some teams would be idle while others were very busy and this would be an inefficient way of employing labour and equipment (see part (a) of the figure on the next page). Toyota therefore distributes production evenly throughout the day in the assembly process (see part (b) of the figure). This means that Toyota can get by with a

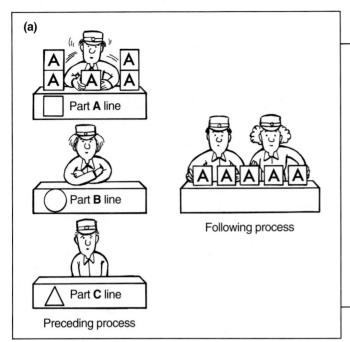

(a) *Conventional production systems concentrate work on different processes at different times.*

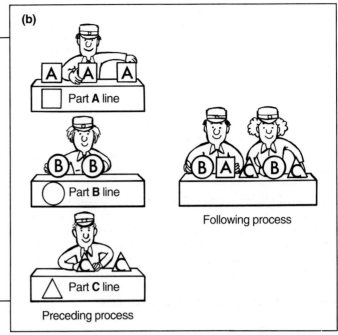

((b) Heijunka *levelled production distributes work evenly among the steps in the production sequence at all times.*

minimum of labour and equipment in the assembly processes, the preceding manufacturing processes and in the transport that takes place between processes. For *heijunka* to work properly, therefore, the workers, production and inspection equipment and the transport system between processes must be capable of handling the variety of tasks and items involved in different model types. Toyota therefore trains its workers in a range of jobs and skills and develops equipment and transport capacity that gives it the flexibility to handle the different kinds of work associated with *heijunka*. *Heijunka* sequential planning goes into effect at the start of body production. The vehicles then proceed more or less in that same sequence through the production process – from welding to painting, through assembly to finally leaving the plant.

Continuous flow processing

Heijunka and the *kanban* system help to produce a smooth flow of work in and between the different stages of the overall production sequence. To maximize efficiency, however, the production processes themselves must also be arranged into a single continuous flow so that work moves smoothly one piece at a time. As far as possible, sub-assembly flows must be integrated into the main assembly lines so that every kind of process becomes part of an overall production flow that allows work to progress smoothly. The layout of plants is therefore determined by the need to produce and sustain this continuous flow and this involves arranging equipment in accordance with the production sequence. At one time equipment was grouped separately according to process or kind of machine. This was found to prevent a smooth flow and had several disadvantages:

- work in progress collecting after each machine and process;
- a great deal of movement and transporting between processes;
- a greater amount of material handling by an operator than was necessary;

- long production lead times and also a poor response to changes in specifications;
- defective items not immediately becoming apparent and corrective action getting delayed;
- operators only acquiring the skills relating to their particular occupation, resulting in the need for a larger workforce.

The high levels of activity at each machine and the collection of work in progress gave the impression that the factory as a whole was very busy and that everything being produced was actually needed to meet what appeared to be healthy orders from customers. Furthermore, the work flow, production sequence and the kind of work carried out by employees meant that they were relatively isolated from each other and had little or no knowledge of other processes. The system did not, therefore, readily lend itself to the involvement of teams in establishing standardized work to maintain productivity, high quality and safe working methods.

Continuous flow processing, involving one-at-a-time production, is not practical in work where there is a need to change dies, moulds or other tools to produce different items on the same equipment such as in forging, casting and moulding. Under these circumstances, batch production will be undertaken. Even here, however, Toyota still seeks to raise efficiency by continually finding ways of introducing some of the principles of continuous flow processing into batch production. For instance, it is possible to arrange six stamping machines in a row – from first step to sixth – to process material one piece at a time in a continuous flow. Presses and moulding machines used in batch production tend to be very large and are generally installed and operated in separate shops away from the assembly line. Toyota, however, continues to develop smaller machines that allow more of this kind of work to be installed in the most appropriate place alongside the assembly line. Having located processes and equipment in order to achieve a continuous smooth flow, their exact positioning is then determined in

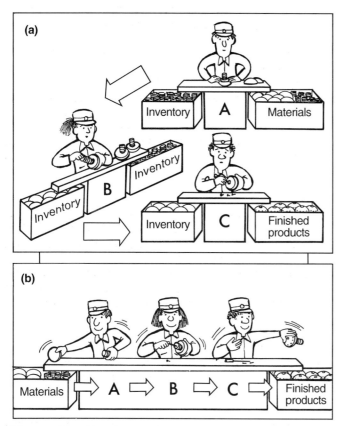

(a) Separately positioned processing.
(b) Continuous-flow processing.

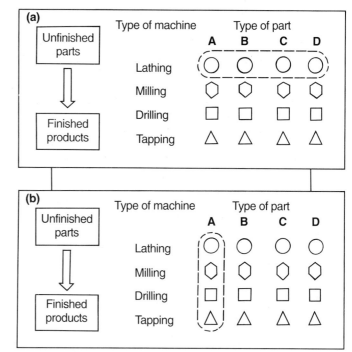

(a) Multi-machine handling: one person handles four machines of the same type.
(b) Multi-process handling: one person handles four different types of machines.

order to maximize efficiency. Machines should be as close together as possible to minimize the movement of items between them. Isolated job sites should be avoided.

Toyota has recognized another important factor that needs to be considered when using batch production: the value of using the smallest possible batches. Batch production usually involves changing dies and other tools and fittings to produce different items with the same machine. Setting the machine up to produce a different item is time-consuming, and manufacturers have generally opted for large batches to compensate for the long setting-up time. This, however, produces large stocks alongside the batch-processing machines and also in the preceding stages of production that supply those machines. Toyota therefore seeks to minimize stocks of work in progress and increase flexibility by reducing the size of batches. For example, if it needs 1,000 units each of parts A and B from the same machine, then rather than two batches of 1,000, it will perhaps produce them in four lots of 500 and protect productivity by finding ways to shorten the setting-up time for the different dies and moulds.

This method of working affects the way in which Toyota allocates work to its employees. Manufacturers traditionally sought to improve efficiency by making individual employees responsible for several machines of the same type. An example of this can be seen in part (a) of the following diagram. The process starts with a lathe operator who processes four parts on four lathes. These parts are then passed on to a milling machine operator who then processes them on four milling machines. The parts then move on to drilling and tapping in the same way. This 'multi-machine handling' means that the part the lathe

operator processes on the first lathe remains there until the parts on the other three lathes have also been processed. This gives rise to long lead times and frequent overproduction, and the exact circumstances surrounding a defective item will be difficult to identify.

In contrast to this, Toyota seeks to process work using 'multi-process handling'. This is where an employee is trained so that he or she operates different kinds of machines to move items through a processing system one at a time. This is represented in part (b) of the diagram, where one operator uses a lathe, a milling machine, a drill and then a tapping machine on each item in sequence. Multi-process handling is vital for JIT production as it avoids a build-up of work in progress and ensures that the item needed in the following stage exactly meets requirements and is readily available. Toyota now designs and locates machines and equipment in ways that allow for multi-process handling.

Activities

Short answer questions

1   What are the disadvantages of holding large stocks of raw materials and parts?

2   Why will the kanban used by Toyota avoid the accumulation of excessive stocks beside the assembly line and of work in progress?

3   List the reasons why the money spent on a technology that identifies faults and abnormalities is a worthwhile investment.

4   What kinds of problems can arise if, in dealing with a problem, a motor vehicle assembly line comes to a halt when employees are still engaged in their particular operations?

5 Why is it important for certain aspects of Toyota's kaizen activities that employees are trained to use different kinds of machinery?

6 After the improvement to eliminate unnecessary waiting, shown in the figure on page 58, why will the operator have to commence the process with workpieces ready for each machine, e.g. having started machine A and moved to machine B. There must be a workpiece at that position which has already passed through machine A.

7 All the different parts dealt with by the individual workers in the figure on page 59 have to pass through the same following process. What are the advantages of levelled production for the workers in all processes?

8 List the advantages produced by the shift to continuous flow processing illustrated in the figure in the left-hand column of page 60 in connection with handling, work in progress, identifying causes of faults, balancing the distribution of work between employees and shifting to a different kind of assembly.

Case study 1: The Toyota Motor Corporation in the UK

In 1989, Toyota announced plans to build a vehicle manufacturing plant in Burnaston, Derbyshire, and an engine plant in Deeside, North Wales. It gave the following reasons for locating its first European manufacturing plants in the UK:

1 the UK has a reasonably sized domestic market;
2 there is a tradition of vehicle manufacture in the UK, including a significant parts and components sector;
3 the UK offers good access to the rest of Europe;
4 both national government and local authorities have a cooperative attitude.

Toyota considered many sites in the UK but chose Burnaston because:

1 it offered a large site with room for expansion;
2 the links with the rest of the UK, particularly by road, are good;
3 other infrastructure, such as electricity, gas and water, is easy to obtain;
4 the area offers a large and skilled workforce, experienced in high-quality engineering.

The engine plant is on a separate site because:

1 it has different strategic needs and can develop its own character;
2 it requires different skills and production processes;
3 it has a longer product life cycle;
4 management at both plants can develop their own systems and operating technologies to improve quality and productivity and generally implement the features of the Toyota Production System.

Production at Burnaston started in 1993 with the Carina E but it was planned to add the 'liftback' model, and by 1995 output was expected to reach 100,000 vehicles with a workforce of 3,000 compared with 1,143 in 1993. It is estimated that 70 per cent of output will be exported. The Welsh engine plant would eventually employ 300 people. The proportion of European components in the cars was expected to rise from 60 per cent in 1993 to 80 per cent by mid-1995. There are 160 component and parts suppliers spread across ten European countries and thirty-six raw material suppliers in the UK and Europe. Major supplies from UK companies include steel sheet from British Steel, paint from PPG, drive shafts from GKN, batteries from Lucas and tyres from Dunlop. The parts warehouse and distribution centre is in Lutterworth, Leicestershire, and the vehicle distribution and import centre is in Sheerness. At the end of 1991 there were 230 dealers but this was expected to rise to 400 by 1994.

Tasks

1 Locate Burnaston and Deeside on a detailed road atlas of the UK. What locational advantages do these sites offer?

2 Comment upon the choice of Lutterworth and Sheerness for their respective activities.

3 Find out how central and local government authorities attract foreign companies to the UK, and how this might be assisted by membership of the European Community.

Case study 2

The following diagram shows a jidoka improvement for preventing workpieces with a missing nut from progressing further in the production sequence.

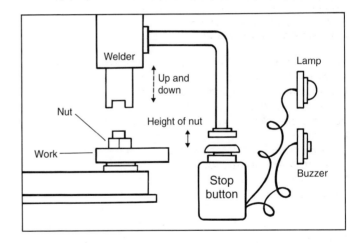

Tasks

1 Explain how the device works.
2 Describe the possible implications of not having such devices.

Local Investigation

Students should organize themselves into small groups and each group should then identify a different company in its local area involved in manufacturing and/or assembly. Useful sources may be the Yellow Pages and newspapers that advertise vacancies or personal contacts. Each group should then arrange a visit to their company in order to produce a brief written or oral report that answers the following questions:

1 What are the products used for and who are their customers?

2   How is production organized: i.e. unit-, batch- or mass-production?

3   What kinds of operations or processes are carried out – e.g. casting, moulding, pressing, forging, rolling, extruding, milling, cutting, drilling, tapping, assembly, etc. – and to what extent is continuous flow processing employed?

4   How is handling between sections or operations carried out?

5   To what extent do workers use a variety of machinery or equipment?

6   How is quality control organized?

7   Has any machinery or equipment that incorporates a new technology recently been introduced?

8   To what degree are the kinds of skills used readily available in the local labour market?

From the outset, all groups should also carry out a survey of the local labour market over a period of four weeks, in order to assess manufacturing and assembly vacancies as a percentage of all vacancies and to determine how the former are split between the various kinds of manual jobs found in manufacturing and assembly. The results should be used in connection with question 8 above.

Financial management
Sainsbury's

7

Introduction

The Sainsbury's Group runs one of the most successful retailing operations within Britain. In the year to 1993 its sales exceeded those of any other British retailer and its profits made Sainsbury's the most profitable retailer in Britain. Around 90 per cent of the Group's sales are through its chain of 328 supermarkets.

A Sainsbury's supermarket, Rustington

The remaining business is generated by its three retailing subsidiaries.

A Savacentre hypermarket, London Colney, Hertfordshire

Savacentre is a hypermarket company which was formed in 1975 and operates nine stores. These hypermarkets offer 60,000 products under one roof covering fresh food, groceries, toiletries, clothing, household goods, lighting, electrical appliances, and home improvement and gardening products.

Homebase is a chain of seventy home improvement and garden centres which was set up in 1979 with the Belgian company GB-Inno-BM as a minority shareholder.

A Homebase house and garden centre, Upton, Wirral.

Shaw's is a chain of seventy-nine supermarkets operating in the USA. Shaw's became part of the Sainsbury Group in 1987.

A Shaw's supermarket, Keene, New Hampshire.

Growth and development

The first shop

The first Sainsbury's shop was a dairy. It opened in 1869 in London's Drury Lane and sold butter, milk and eggs. The business was founded by Mary Ann and John James Sainsbury and in spite of the considerable growth of the business the Sainsbury family is still closely involved in its running. David Sainsbury is the present chairman.

Growth of the business

Initially the business developed within London's Kentish Town and Islington, but subsequently the Sainsbury family recognized the market potential of middle-class suburbs such as Croydon, Balham and Lewisham. By the turn of the century the company had forty-eight shops throughout London and the South-East. They stocked a much wider range of goods including cooked meats, bacon and hams.

In the 1920s, grocery departments were introduced and a new range of Sainsbury-brand grocery lines was launched.

Throughout the 1930s the company expanded steadily and by 1939 Sainsbury's had a chain of 250 shops with an average sales area of 2,200 square feet per shop. The shops sold dairy produce, poultry and game, cooked meats, bacon and hams, fresh meat and groceries.

Changing fortunes

Food rationing, stricter building controls and the effects of evacuation and bombing in the South-East severely damaged Sainsbury's trading position, both during and immediately after the Second World War.

The introduction of self-service in 1950 at Croydon and the opening of the first supermarket at Southampton in 1954 heralded an improvement in Sainsbury's fortunes. By 1970 almost 50 per cent of Sainsbury's branches were supermarkets.

The volume of sales enjoyed by Sainsbury's increased significantly, because large self-service stores could offer a much wider range of goods, including beers, wines and spirits, hardware and textiles. In fact between 1970 and 1991 the number of products offered by Sainsbury's increased from fewer than 4,000 to over 15,000.

The further expansion of the company was aided by its decision to go public in 1973. However, the Sainsbury family and its charitable trust retained the major shareholding and members of the family continued to be actively involved in running the business.

Embracing modern trends

The implications of wider car ownership, with the resulting increase in shopping by car, were recognized by Sainsbury's in the early 1970s. In 1972 Sainsbury's opened its first edge-of-town supermarket at Bretton near Peterborough. This provided good access and plenty of surface level parking. In 1974 Sainsbury's started to complement this development by placing petrol stations on edge-of-town sites. By the early 1990s over two-thirds of Sainsbury's customers were able to shop by car.

Continual expansion

During the past fifty years the geographical trading area covered by Sainsbury's has gradually expanded out from London and the

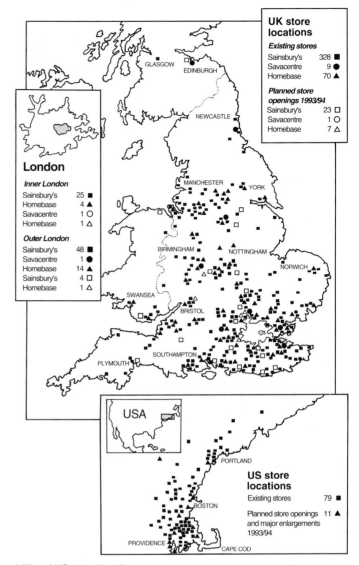

UK and US store locations.

South-East into the Midlands, the North-East and the North-West.

The maps above clearly indicate the spread of retailing activities of the Sainsbury's Group. They also demonstrate how the Group is constantly looking towards the future and considering other areas for expansion.

From its modest beginnings as a single shop, Sainsbury's now serves some 7.5 million customers through its supermarkets and hypermarkets and 9.5 million across the Group as a whole. An operation of this size can only function efficiently if it is underpinned by tight financial management and control.

The general role of financial management in the service and manufacturing sectors

A retail organization as large as Sainsbury's obviously has its own approach to financial management. Before analysing this in detail it is important to clarify certain points about the role of financial management in business in general.

The individual or department that takes responsibility for the financial management of any business has to record and monitor the business's financial dealings and provide financial information or analysis to other parts of the business, or to the Government, or to members of society. In the modern business world financial management is very complex and so for a medium-to-large company it will generally be necessary to employ a number of accountants with differing specialisms: namely, a financial accountant, a cost accountant and a management accountant.

The financial accountant

The financial accountant's main role is to prepare accounts by basic book-keeping methods and to distribute those accounts to other members of the company, to the shareholders and to the creditors. This will allow them to measure the financial position and progress of the business and where relevant to plan for the future. The three main accounting reports that the financial accountant has to prepare are:

1   the Trading and Profit and Loss Account, which effectively establishes whether a profit or loss has been made during the accounting period;
2   the Profit and Loss Appropriation Account, which shows how the net profit has been shared amongst the shareholders;
3   the company Balance sheet, which lists the assets and liabilities of a business at the Balance Sheet date.

Under the provision of the 1985 Companies Act as amended by the 1989 Act, it is a legal requirement for a company to have its accounts audited by a team of professional auditors. It is also necessary to incorporate these three accounting reports into the Annual Report and Accounts, which is filed at Companies House, distributed to shareholders and made available to the general public.

The Annual Report and Accounts generally cover the following items:

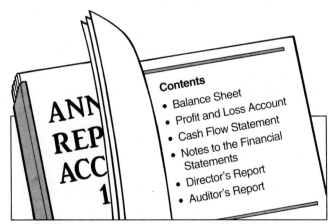

Coverage of the Annual Report and Accounts.

The first two items have already been explained above. The Cash Flow Statement shows the movement of cash in and out of the business during the year. It covers operating activities, returns on investments and servicing of finance, taxation, investing activities and financing. The Notes to the Financial Statements give details of the accounting policies used for calculating the first three items.

The Director's Report gives the information required by law on the shareholders and their shareholdings; details of the proposed dividend, directors' remuneration; number of employees; a statement of the company's performance during the year and a forecast of the company's probable performance in the future. In many cases it is supported by a statement from the chairman as to the overall progress of the company during the year and its future strategy.

The Auditors' Report indicates whether the accounts give a true and fair view of the company's position and whether the accounts satisfy the needs of the Companies Act.

Over recent years there has been a general move by some companies (but not Sainsbury's) not to send out a full set of accounts to their shareholders, because this is expensive and felt to be unnecessary as shareholders do not always read them through. As a cheaper alternative a Summary Financial Statement may be used. This has to provide summaries of the Profit and Loss Account and the Balance Sheet; and the Directors' Report; and a statement by the company's auditors on whether the summary is consistent with the accounts.

Because of the rapid changes that occur within the business environment, one document representing a year's results does not provide sufficient information to gauge and monitor a company's performance. Therefore, to aid senior management in its decision making and to keep directors informed, the financial accountant often provides the management and directors with monthly accounting information and issues a half-yearly (interim) statement.

To secure an even more detailed picture, financial analysts are often employed to make monthly and year-on-year comparisons of the company's performance. This allows management to diagnose potential problems, highlight new opportunities and project future trends. Much of this analysis may incorporate the use of various ratios. The standard ratios generally employed are shown in the box below.

Standard accounting ratios
Profitability

By expressing profits as a ratio against some other factor it is possible to derive a comparative figure (normally expressed in percentage terms) by which the level of success of a business may be measured. The most common ways of doing this are as follows:

4   gross profit margin (%) $= \dfrac{\text{gross profit}}{\text{sales}} \times 100$

5   mark-up on cost (%) $= \dfrac{\text{gross profit}}{\text{cost of goods sold}} \times 100$

6   net profit margin (%) $= \dfrac{\text{net profit}}{\text{sales}} \times 100$

The ratios may be used when making comparisons over time, or when comparing the relative performance of two companies, or when comparing the performance of a company against a target.

A more realistic measurement of performance is the following:

7   return on capital employed (%) $= \dfrac{\text{net profit}}{\text{capital employed}}$

The advantage of this ratio is that it indicates what the business has actually returned on its assets. This may be put into context by considering what might have been achieved if the capital had been employed in some other way; for example, left in the bank.

Liquidity

These ratios determine whether the company is solvent, that is, able to pay its debts. This may be measured in two ways:

8   current or working capital ratio = $\dfrac{\text{current assets}}{\text{current liabilities}}$

If this is around 2:1 then the company is generally considered to be quite safe. If it is much higher than 2.5:1 then this would suggest the company is not being managed properly and it is not making the best use of its assets.

An alternative, tougher measurement that really reflects whether the business can cover its liabilities is the Acid Test, which is expressed as:

9   acid test ratio = $\dfrac{\text{current assets} - \text{stock}}{\text{current liabilities}}$

This needs to be about 1:1. If it is very much less than this then the business is in danger of not being able to cover its debts. If the ratio is significantly greater than 1:1, then the business may be considered not to be making the best use of its funds.

Activity

One of the measurements that may be used is the volume of trade undertaken. A good measurement of this may be the rate at which stock is sold within a given period (usually one year).

10   rate of stock turnover = $\dfrac{\text{cost of goods sold}}{\text{average stock}}$

This provides a useful figure to compare with other businesses or time periods on a particular target.

The cost accountant

The cost accountant deals with the costing of selected products or services. This is done by putting estimates to a unit (a unit being a process of production) and therefore building a standard. This is invaluable to an organization when attempts are being made to deal with actual costs. The resulting analysis can be used to help to decide which products to specialize in, what price to sell at and at what level of output or unit of service the business would break even.

Most manufacturing organizations today employ the principle of standard costing. The principle hinges on the identification and classification of costs. Input costs can be either direct or indirect. An example of direct costs would be labour and materials, which can be fairly easily identified. What cannot be easily identified are the indirect costs. For example, the overall costs of heating, lighting and rent cannot be attached directly and solely to a job or process. A system has to be established,

therefore, by which the cost may be allocated or spread between different jobs. There are various ways of doing this. For example, heating might be allocated or apportioned according to floor space, whereas insurance would be apportioned according to the capital value of equipment used. Depending on whether the manufacturing process is labour- or machine-orientated, the total collection of these costs and the total machine hours or labour hours would form a standard labour overhead rate or a standard machine overhead rate.

These standard rates are then compared with the actual costs incurred, and consideration of any differences through variance analysis then aids management decision making by flagging potential problem areas. For example, variances in the labour rate may suggest that there has been a change in the actual wage rate or a difference in the time taken to complete the job. This may prompt management to investigate methods of payment and the quality and productivity of the workforce. Variance analysis can therefore help to highlight inefficiencies, aid cost production and suggest performance techniques and productivity agreements that help to smooth out these inefficiencies.

The cost accountant has a close relationship with all departments concerned with manufacturing. The costs are incurred from the time the materials are bought to the time they are issued to production and to the time they are made into complete units. These departments provide the cost accountant with the necessary facts and figures. The cost accountant must analyse these figures and present them to the management of those departments so that the information can be used as an aid to better decision making.

The management accountant

The management accountant essentially produces information for internal use. Such information is usually more detailed, and more promptly and frequently prepared than financial accounts. The main aspects of the management accountant's work are budgeting and investment appraisal of capital projects. In certain cases the work of the cost accountant may be included under management accounting.

Basically, management accounting originates from the company's overall business plan. This may project the position of the company three to five years into the future. Such planning is a difficult process in itself and there are basic rules and guidelines that need to be adhered to. For instance, one of the problems is that planning is not responsive enough to latest events and therefore it is most important to state the basis for the plan and the date when it was issued.

Budgeting is an integral part of the planning process. It provides an essential form of financial control. The various stages of budgetary control are shown on the opposite page.

It should be remembered that, during periods of inflation and environmental uncertainty, a budget should not be treated with rigidity but should be flexible in its approach. This will reduce the danger of management being restricted in its actions and unable either to take advantage of market opportunities or to reflect economic downturns.

Investment appraisal is a major aspect of the management accountant's work. Basically, this involves deciding upon whether a proposed project is worth investing in. This will be determined by the returns and costs associated with a particular project and how these are likely to be influenced by the inflation rate.

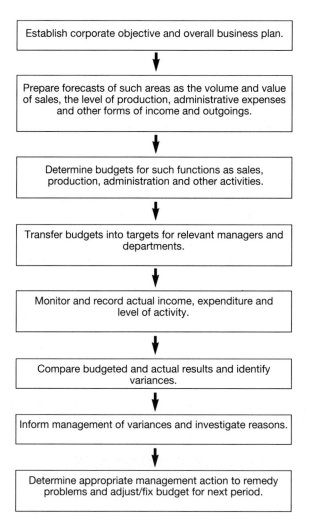

Establish corporate objective and overall business plan.

↓

Prepare forecasts of such areas as the volume and value of sales, the level of production, administrative expenses and other forms of income and outgoings.

↓

Determine budgets for such functions as sales, production, administration and other activities.

↓

Transfer budgets into targets for relevant managers and departments.

↓

Monitor and record actual income, expenditure and level of activity.

↓

Compare budgeted and actual results and identify variances.

↓

Inform management of variances and investigate reasons.

↓

Determine appropriate management action to remedy problems and adjust/fix budget for next period.

Stages of budgetary control.

The Sainsbury's approach to financial management

The Sainsbury's organization has to operate its financial management system at a number of levels: individual branch, company, Group, and across different product areas. Some financial management activities are unique to a particular level. For example, the progress of each branch is monitored through its own profit and loss account. Similarly, reports are produced that provide information on the profitability of particular product areas. Other financial management activities go across all four levels. Sainsbury's has an Accounting Systems Implementation and Testing function, which might investigate a new computer-based accounting system, for example, and assess how it might contribute to the overall Sainsbury's operation. Basically, Sainsbury's financial management activities are concerned with producing multi-tiered financial information that allows line managers to manage more efficiently.

Financial accounting

The activities of the financial accountants are largely reflected in the Annual Report and Accounts. These are built up through recording the activities of the branch and of the company, and

they also reflect the full position of the Group. They consolidate the Group accounts by combining the accounts of J Sainsbury plc, all its Subsidiaries and the relevant Associates. (An Associate is a company in which the Group exercises a significant influence over operating and financial policy and has a participating interest of between 20 and 50 per cent.) The accounts are audited by Clark Whitehill, one of the major firms of Chartered Accountants and Registered Auditors. They verify that the accounts are prepared in accordance with the Companies Act 1985.

CONTENTS

A list of the contents of the Sainsbury's Annual Report and Accounts 1993 is shown above. As can be seen, in addition to publishing financial information, the company uses the document as a public relations and promotional opportunity. It provides a great deal of information about the growth, development and achievements of Sainsbury's. This is particularly true of the Chairman's Statement, which gives considerable coverage to the performance of the Group and how it intends to take advantage of market opportunities for new stores, further develop its own brand, and capitalize on developments in the law regarding Sunday shopping.

The major financial information is included on the Balance Sheet, Profit and Loss Account and Cash Flow Statement, which are shown on the following page.

The Balance Sheet shows both the Group and company positions. The Group column consolidates the entire activities of the Group, including the subsidiaries. In the case of both the Group and the company, the tangible fixed assets refer to properties,

(a)

	1993 £m	1992 £m
Group Sales (including		
VAT & Sales Taxes)	10,269.7	9,202.3
VAT & Sales Taxes	584.2	506.8
Group Sales (excluding		
VAT & Sales Taxes)	9,685.5	8,695.5
Cost of Sales	8,688.9	7,826.7
Gross Profit	996.6	868.8
Administrative		
Expenses	211.6	202.8
Group Operating Profit	785.0	666.0
Associates - share		
of (loss)/profit	(0.4)	1.2
Profit Sharing	(58.6)	(49.4)
Loss on sale of		
properties	(2.4)	(2.5)
Profit on Ordinary		
Activities before Interest	723.6	615.3
Net interest receivable	9.2	12.7
Profit on Ordinary		
Activities before Tax	732.8	628.0
Tax on Profit on		
Ordinary Activities	228.8	184.5
Profit on Ordinary		
Activities after Tax	504.0	443.5
Minority Interest	1.2	5.3
Profit for Financial Year	502.8	438.2
Dividends	177.3	153.7
Profit Retained	325.5	284.5
Earnings per Share	28.47p	25.69p
Fully Diluted Earnings		
per Share	27.94p	25.22p
Adjustment for loss		
on sale of properties	0.13p	0.12p
Fully Diluted Earnings		
per Share (excluding		
loss on sale of		
properties)	28.07p	25.34p

Sainsbury's Annual Report and Accounts 1993: (a) Profit and Loss Account; (b) Balance Sheet; (c) Cash Flow

(b)

	Group 1993 £m	Group 1992 £m	Company 1993 £m	Company 1992 £m
Fixed Assets				
Tangible Assets	4,448.5	3,809.2	3,662.0	3,123.5
Investments	29.4	27.6	624.9	574.7
	4,477.9	3836.8	4,286.9	3,698.2
Current Assets				
Investments	78.5	189.6	78.5	139.2
Stocks	448.2	386.5	261.0	229.1
Debtors	95.3	80.8	56.1	63.0
ACT Recoverable	37.6	37.3	37.6	37.3
Cash at Bank and in Hand	144.4	173.9	90.7	87.6
	804.0	868.1	523.9	556.2
Creditors: due within one year	(1,524.6)	(1,468.2)	(1,319.5)	(1,274.5)
Net Current Liabilities	(720.6)	(600.1)	(795.6)	(718.3)
Total Assets Less Current Liabilities	3,757.3	3,236.7	3,491.3	2,979.9
Creditors: due after one year				
Convertible	(200.0)	(200.0)	–	–
Other	(513.2)	(377.9)	(674.0)	(478.9)
Deferred Tax	2.0	(1.7)	9.4	5.5
Minority Interest	(17.4)	(16.2)	–	–
	3,028.7	2,640.9	2,826.7	2,506.5
Capital and Reserves				
Called up Share Capital	443.7	439.4	443.7	439.4
Share Premium Account	895.4	837.5	895.4	837.5
Revaluation Reserve	26.8	26.8	28.1	28.1
Profit and Loss Account	1,662.8	1,337.2	1,459.5	1,201.5
	3,028.7	2,640.9	2,826.7	2,506.5

(c)

	1993 £m	1992 £m
Net cash inflow from operating activities	973.2	787.1
Returns on investment and servicing of finance		
Interest received	35.1	111.2
Interest paid	(64.2)	(144.6)
Interest element of finance lease rental payments	(7.3)	(6.9)
Dividends paid	(132.1)	(115.1)
Net case outflow from returns on investments and servicing of finance	(168.5)	(155.4)
Taxation		
Corporation tax paid	(171.8)	(124.9)
Overseas tax paid	(7.6)	(6.8)
Tax paid	(179.4)	(131.7)
Investing activities		
Payments for tangible fixed assets	(741.7)	(707.6)
Receipts from sale of tangible fixed assets	50.5	72.1
Sale/(Purchase) of short-term investments	109.7	(190.9)
Net Investment in Associates	0.4	(6.0)
Net case outflow from all investing activities	(581.1)	(832.4)
Net cash inflow/(outflow) before financing	44.2	(332.4)
Financing		
Issue of ordinary share capital	19.0	509.8
Expenses of capital issues	(0.8)	(6.1)
Proceeds of long-term borrowing	86.1	93.0
Repayment of long-term borrowing	(111.8)	(144.8)
Capital element of finance lease rental payments	(0.7)	(0.5)
Net case inflow/(outflow) from financing	(8.2)	451.4
Increase in cash and cash equivalents	36.0	119.0

fixtures, equipment and vehicles.

The debtors are largely made up of those arising out of trade and amounts owed by subsidiaries. The major creditors are trade creditors.

The Profit and Loss Account and Cash Flow Statement relate to just the Group's activities, which is allowable under the 1985 Companies Act. In the case of the Profit and Loss Account, 97.1 per cent of sales in 1993 came from food retailing.

These three accounts or statements help to provide a picture of the overall performance of the Sainsbury's Group. There will be an opportunity to analyse this in the activities at the end of this unit.

Cost accounting

Cost accounting activities are largely concerned with recording, monitoring and analysing the cost of achieving a sale. This includes all the costs up to the point of sale, including warehousing, transportation and the costs of operating the actual supermarket, such as labour, heating, lighting and rent. These are regularly monitored and compared with the standard and any significant variance investigated so that management may be alerted and the appropriate action taken.

Management accounting

The management accountants have to operate at a number of levels. The Group has an overall business plan with identifiable objectives. These objectives are, broadly stated, to achieve quality and innovation by generating sufficient profit to finance continual improvement and growth of the business while providing the shareholder with a good return on investment. This means that it is necessary to continue to open new branches and to replace or update existing ones. This requires very careful budgetary planning and control. For example, there may be a project to upgrade a store by including a coffee shop. A project manager will be appointed who estimates the costs, issues contracts and supervises the work. The accountant's role is to manage the budget and to report whether the project is either overspent or underspent. The accountant also has to ensure that invoices are paid when they are due and that the costs are allocated correctly to capital or revenue.

With around twenty new stores opening each year, Sainsbury's financial analysts are constantly having to conduct appropriate investment appraisals. For example, in the 1992–3 financial year Sainsbury's opened twenty-three new supermarkets and closed eight older stores, giving a new increase in sales area of 671,000 square feet. Each new store development undergoes rigorous appraisal before the decision to proceed can be made. Careful account has to be taken of the wider local demand factors, such as demographic trends, socioeconomic groups, income levels and the competition. These factors are taken into account along with the costs of the site, of conversion or construction, and fittings and equipment. Ultimately, these cost figures are compared with a minimum acceptable return before a decision is made.

The importance of this investment appraisal can be appreciated by the size of capital expenditure, which is shown in the following chart. The types of project involved can be clearly seen in the photograph beneath it of the Edinburgh store at Blackhall, which was Sainsbury's second supermarket in Scotland and part of the drive into new trading areas.

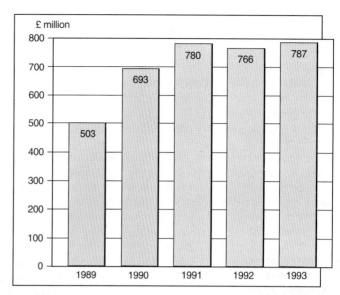

Group capital expenditure totalled £787 million, 75 per cent of which was spent on Sainsbury's store development.

New store development.

Activities

Short-answer questions

1 Explain why the growth of Sainsbury's has necessitated the parallel development within the Group of more sophisticated financial management systems.
2 Suggest how Sainsbury's unit sales costs would have been influenced by the geographical expansion of the company throughout the UK.
3 Suggest the groups that Sainsbury's Annual Report and Accounts are targeted at. Why would they be interested in its contents?
4 Describe the possible impact of inflation on Sainsbury's budgetary approach to the building of an edge-of-town supermarket.
5 How does Sainsbury's use the Annual Report and Accounts as a promotional tool?
6 What business activities are covered in Sainsbury's Annual Report and Accounts?
7 To what extent did Sainsbury's performance improve between 1992 and 1993?

Data assignment

You are employed as a financial analyst in Sainsbury's Group accounting operation. As part of an ongoing review of Sainsbury's financial position you are asked to calculate suitable standard ratios relating to profitability, performance and liquidity. (Use the information contained in the tables on page 68 and select one ratio in each case.)

Local study

As part of its expansion plans, a major supermarket chain is considering the possibility of increasing its number of edge-of-town supermarkets. Assume that you are a member of the team carrying out the investment appraisal. One of the areas selected is your home town. Prior to a full investment analysis you are asked to conduct a preliminary review of the area.

1 Identify a possible site and find out how much it would cost. (This may be carried out as a group or class exercise.)
2 Contact a number of local construction companies and estimate the cost of site clearance, construction and fittings. (This may be carried out in groups.)
3 Gather information from the local area regarding the number of households, average income, shopping habits, car ownership and possible competition. (A questionnaire may be used.)
4 Present your findings in a brief report to your head of department.

Media assignment

Study the extract below from the Chairman's Statement and the financial highlights on the opposite page from Sainsbury's 1993 Report and Accounts.

Adopt the role of an assistant in the finance department of Sainsbury's. The company has a policy of keeping its staff informed about the performance of the business. In order to achieve this objective it is decided that a newsletter should be circulated to all employees highlighting the performance of the company during the past financial year. You are given the task of designing the newsletter. It should comprise two sides of A4 paper, charts and diagrams should be used whenever possible and technical language should be avoided.

CHAIRMAN'S STATEMENT

Sainsbury's has always been inspired by a passion for quality and innovation, and a commitment to providing outstanding value for money to our customers. These continuing objectives have enabled us to grow and prosper in fiercely competitive retail sectors, whatever the market conditions. In this my first annual statement as your Chairman, I am pleased to report that Sainsbury's has again achieved an outstanding performance, and that we have increased our lead over our principal competitors.

Group profit before tax increased by 16.7% to £732.8 million and Group sales exceeded £10 billion for the first time. Sainsbury's and our retail subsidiaries now serve over ten million customers each week, and our increasing sales and market shares testify to our success in providing quality and value. We benchmark our performance, our skills and our technology against the best food retailers in the world, and we believe that we are at the leading edge of world food retailing.

We continue to invest for the future. Group capital investment totalled £787 million and Group return on capital employed remained stable at 21.5%, a satisfactory level in view of the scale of our investment programme. At the end of the year net Group borrowing amounted to 18.7% of shareholders' funds. This low level of gearing places us in a very strong financial position for the future.

Retail performance

Sales in Sainsbury's supermarkets and Savacentre hypermarkets increased by 12.6% to £8.9 billion, and market share grew by 0.7 percentage points to 11.3%. This increase in sales was achieved at a time when sales inflation of 2.5% was at its lowest level for six years. New stores performed well and, net of closures, contributed just over two-thirds of the total sales increase. Sales in existing stores grew by 3.8% reflecting the value of the Sainsbury's offer and the extension of Sunday shopping. Sainsbury's price competitiveness improved during the period and on average the prices paid by our customers were over 2% less than they would have paid in other large supermarket retailers.

Operating profit for Sainsbury's and Savacentre increased by 19.1% to £752.2 million as a result of strong sales and a tight control of costs. Sales per full-time equivalent employee increased by 6.3% while, at the same time, customer service standards were improved. We see many opportunities for improving the performance of the business and in the next two years we will enhance our efficiency and customer service by implementing several major new computer systems.

Homebase achieved considerable success in highly competitive market conditions. Homebase's sales increased by 9.8% to £283 million and operating profit by 16.3% to £17.8 million. Seven new stores opened in the year, and the total number of Homebase stores increased to 70.

Shaw's suffered adversely from the continuing recession in the New England economy now in its third year, and its profitability was also affected by the costs of new developments which will aid growth in the longer term. Shaw's sales increased by 2% to $1.85 billion while operating profits fell by 11.9% to $31.5 million. In the second half, Shaw's sales increased by 4% and operating profits were at the same level as in the previous year. The benefits of our investment in Shaw's own brand and new systems are now becoming evident, and seven new stores were opened during the year.

FINANCIAL HIGHLIGHTS

£ million	1993 52 weeks to 13 March	1992 52 weeks to 14 March	% change
UK sales	9,179.1	8,159.2	12.5
US sales	1,090.6	1,043.1	4.6
Group Sales	**10,269.7**	**9,202.3**	**11.6**
UK Operating Profit	766.4	645.4	18.8
US Operating Profit	18.6	20.6	(9.9)
Group Operating Profit	**785.0**	**666.0**	**17.9**
Associates	(0.4)	1.2	
Profit Sharing	(58.6)	(49.4)	
Loss on sale of properties	(2.4)	(2.5)	
Group Profit before Interest	723.6	615.3	17.6
Net Interest Receivable	9.2	12.7	
Group Profit before Tax	**732.8**	**628.0**	**16.7**
Taxation	228.8	184.5	
Group Profit after Tax	504.0	443.5	13.7
Earnings per Share	**28.47p**	**25.69p**	**10.8**
Dividend per Share	**10.00p**	**8.75p**	**14.3**

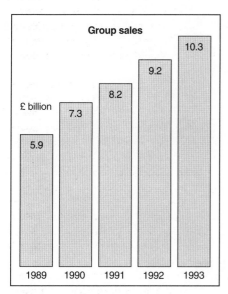

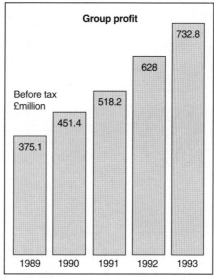

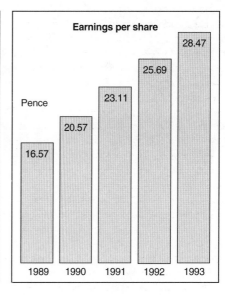

Group sales increased by £1.1 billion (11.6%) to exceed £10 billion. Group profit increased by 16.7% to £732.8 million.
Earnings per share increased by 10.8% to 26.47 pence.

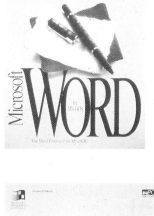

A range of Microsoft's products.

Introduction

The Microsoft Corporation is a global organization that designs, develops, markets and supports a wide range of personal computer systems, applications, development tools and languages, hardware peripherals, books and multimedia applications. Its products are used extensively in industry, commerce, education and the home.

Microsoft's range of products can be used on all the popular microcomputers, such as IBM and IBM-compatible PCs, and Apple Macintoshes.

Growth and development

Origins in Basic

In 1975 in the United States, Bill Gates and Paul Allen completed their development work on adapting the programming language Basic (beginner's all-purpose symbolic instruction code) for use on a personal computer. They then founded Microsoft as a partnership and by July 1976 they had sold Microsoft® Basic to such organizations as General Electric, National Cash Registers (NCR) and Citibank. During the next two years Microsoft developed two further language products: Microsoft® FORTRAN in 1977 and then Microsoft® COBOL for the 8080, Z–80 and 8085 microprocessor systems. Microsoft's products were so successful that by 1979 the Basic compiler had been implemented on virtually every microcomputer that was available.

Microsoft then started to engage in forward vertical integration by founding a Retail Division which targeted household customers. Within two years a national network of retail sales representatives had been established.

Corporate status

In June 1981 Microsoft reorganized its operations as the privately owned Microsoft Corporation, with Bill Gates as President and Chairman of the Board and Paul Allen as the Executive Vice-President. In the same year, wider recognition of its products came when IBM introduced its personal computer, which made use of Microsoft's 16-bit operation system, MS-DOS® version 1.00, plus Microsoft Basic, COBOL, Microsoft® Pascal and other Microsoft products.

In 1981 the Corporation started to expand abroad and set up a UK subsidiary – Microsoft Limited – which represented the beginning of a foreign sales effort.

Growth through diversification

In March 1983, Microsoft formed a book publishing division called Microsoft Press. Within twelve months it had introduced its first two titles: Cary Lu's *The Apple Macintosh Book* and Peter Norton's *Exploring the IBM PCjr Home Computer*.

Further expansion took place in April 1984, when Microsoft created a new Hardware and Peripherals Division to develop and market hardware products that complemented its software product line.

Microsoft also strengthened its position within the recreational market by producing in 1984 an enhanced version of Microsoft® Flight Simulator®, which became the best-selling recreational software package for the IBM PC and compatibles market.

The corporation continued to expand rapidly, and in the 1985 fiscal year, within ten years of its foundation, it achieved sales of $140 million. Also in that year, expansion continued with the setting up in Ireland of Microsoft's first manufacturing facility outside the United States.

Going public

On 13 March 1986 the Corporation went public, which allowed it to sell its shares to the general public. The shares issued at $21.00, and by the end of the first trading day they had risen to $28.00. The initial public offer had raised $61 million.

A world leader

By 1988 Microsoft had become the largest PC software company, as measured by sales, and its international operations had increased to 48 per cent of its total sales. Two years later Microsoft had become the first personal computer software company to exceed $1 billion in sales in a single year.

International operations expanded in 1992 into Malaysia, Finland, Venezuela, South Africa and Russia. By January 1992, Microsoft had become the world's largest computer-industry company measured in terms of market value.

In May 1993 its highly successful Microsoft® Windows™ operating system had its own world trade show. Windows is an easy-to-learn, user-friendly graphical user interface. It uses rectangular areas of the computer screen called 'windows', which appear on a background called the 'desktop'. The 'applications' used (such as word processing or spreadsheet programs) are represented in Windows by small graphical symbols called 'icons'. When an application is opened, by selecting its icon with a pointing device called a 'mouse', it is placed in a window. Several applications can be open at the same time, and it is easy to move from one application to another by selecting different windows. An example of what it is capable of producing is shown below.

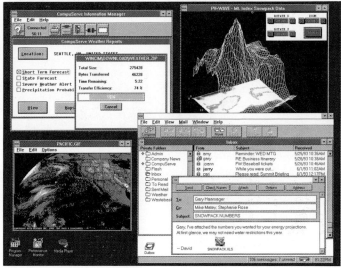

Examples of 32-bit Windows at work: using a high-performance graphics application (upper right); information, files and ideas can be shared quickly and easily using integrated email and networking services (lower right).

The general approach to business planning for change

The Microsoft Corporation is obviously at the very forefront of technological and business change. Before analysing this in detail it is important to clarify certain points about the general approach taken by businesses when planning in a changing environment.

The changing business environment

All businesses operate in a constantly changing business world. From its initial inception and throughout its life a business has to take account of these changes. This is particularly true when it is drawing up its original business plan, developing its marketing strategy or formulating its strategic plan.

The business environment is affected by five main areas of change: economic, demographic and social, legal, political and technological.

Economic change

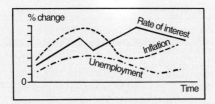

This involves movements in the major economic and financial indicators, such as the rate of inflation, wage and raw material costs, money supply and interest rates, employment, economic growth, investment, balance of payments and exchange rate, public spending, tax rates and the public sector borrowing requirement (PSBR). Changes in these factors will influence the level of activity in the economy and hence business prospects.

Demographic and social change

This involves alterations in the total size, structure and distribution of the population, which are influenced by movements in the birth rate, death rate and rate of migration. It also refers to changes in the composition of the population, including the size and type of household unit and its collective, material and employment needs. These changes reflect shifts in social attitudes, and in such factors as the role of women, marriage and the family.

Legal change

This reflects the creation of new laws or the modification of existing ones. The law has a significant effect on the way in which business is conducted and the treatment of customers and employees.

Political change

This embraces alterations in the constitution and the make-up of the government and political parties. Governments stay in power by taking account of public opinion, pressure group activity and changing national and international circumstances. All of these factors impact upon the business world, sometimes to the extent of changing the very nature of business.

Technological change

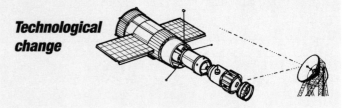

This involves changes in the process by which a product is produced or a service is provided, or developments in the product itself. Businesses have to be constantly researching and developing both their products and methods of production in order to ensure that they stay competitive.

Planning a new business

Change in the business environment has a dual effect. On the one hand it generates business opportunities and on the other it creates threats and pitfalls for both new and existing businesses. The business environment must therefore be constantly scanned for economic, legal, social, political and technological change, and this is as important for budding entrepreneurs as it is for established tycoons. The success of such business people as Richard Branson at Virgin and Alan Sugar at Amstrad is probably due as much to their ability to identify changes in the business world as to their skill at reading a balance sheet. The ability to recognize a business opportunity and then exploit it is the hallmark of a successful entrepreneur.

During the 1980s, an average of half a million businesses started up each year. Generally, 40 per cent failed within the first three years of operation. Much of this failure was due to inadequate planning in a changing business environment.

At its simplest, a business start-up plan is a statement of the basic business idea and its market potential, a description of where the business is to be located, and how it is to be resourced, organized and financed. The banks are only prepared to lend money if a proper business plan has been drawn up. The major questions and issues that the Midland Bank would expect to be covered in any business plan accompanying a request for finance are shown on the following page.

Your business plan

Who you are

- Name, address and telephone number of business.
- Date business commenced.
- Legal status (e.g. sole trader, partnership, limited company).
- Principal activities.

Key personnel

- Details of the key people in the business (names, dates of birth, positions in the business, academic/professional qualifications, experience and knowledge of your industry).
- Details of their previous employment (names of employers, positions held, dates of employment).
- Proposed additions to the present management team (skills required, positions, proposed salaries).
- What contingency plans do you have if you or your key personnel are unable to work through illness or injury? Premises
- Describe your business premises, including size, location and state of repair.
- If freehold, give the value, amount of mortgage outstanding, monthly repayment amount, and name of lender.
- If leasehold, give date the lease expires, whether there is an option to renew, amount of annual rent, date rent is payable, and date of next rent review.
- Uniform business rate: give annual amount and date when payable.
- Insurance: give amount of cover, annual premium, and date when payable.
- Are the premises adequate for your future needs? If not what future plans do you have?
- Any competitive advantage in relation to the premises, its location and your customer base?

Plant, machinery and equipment

- Detail existing plant, machinery and equipment, giving life expectancy and value of each item.
- What capital expenditure do you anticipate during the next 12 months? Give life expenditure and cost of each item.

Products and services

- What are the main products and services offered by your business and what proportion of turnover does each contribute?
- Include any catalogues or promotional brochures with the business plan.
- What further products or services are being developed?
- Who are your key suppliers and what credit terms will they offer you?
- What stock levels are required in your business? Give the cost of raw materials, and finished goods at cost.

Pricing

- What is the basis for calculating your prices?
- How do your prices compare with the competition? Give your price and competitors' price for each product/service.
- If you allow credit terms, state the number of days based on the above list of products and services.

Customers

- Who and where are your potential customers and how many do you have?
- What are the strengths of your business that will influence customer decisions to purchase your products and services?

Competition

- Who are your major competitors and where are they based?
- What are the strengths and weaknesses of your competitors?
- Is the market static, declining, growing or seasonal, and why?

Promotion

- What level of sales do you anticipate: in the next 6 months and in the following 6 months?
- What firm orders are currently in hand: give customer names and amounts.
- What assumptions have been made in making your sales forecasts?
- How do you intend to promote and sell your products and services? Give the cost of each intended method.

Financial projection

- First of all, decide whether your financial projections are to be calculated on an annual or half-yearly basis.
- Calculate your gross profit (A)
  A = Projected sales – direct costs (purchases and labour costs)
- Calculate your gross profit margin (B)
  $B = A/Sales \times 100$
- Calculate your overheads (C)
  Total overheads = the sum of all indirect costs, i.e.: business salaries (including your drawings), rent, rates, light/heat, power, telephone, insurance, maintenance, advertising, bank interest/HP, and other expenses.
- Calculate the turnover required to break even (D)
  $D = C/B \times 100$
- Calculate the monthly turnover to break even (E)
  $E = D/6$ or $D/12$ (depending on basis of calculation)
- Calculate your estimated profit (F)
  $F = (Projected\ sales – D) \times B$

Strategic planning

The rate of change in the business environment has increased the importance of taking a corporate approach to planning. This is referred to as strategic planning: a systematic and comprehensive process of long-range planning which determines the policies and direction of all activities of the business. It is normally conducted by a special planning group at senior executive level. It is expressed in terms of strategic objectives, targets and acceptable levels of quality and performance. Effectively it takes the corporation's mission statement – which explains what the corporation was set up to achieve – and shows how it is to be achieved over the next three to five years. The various aspects of strategic planning are clearly shown below.

Strategic planning may be conducted in one of two ways.

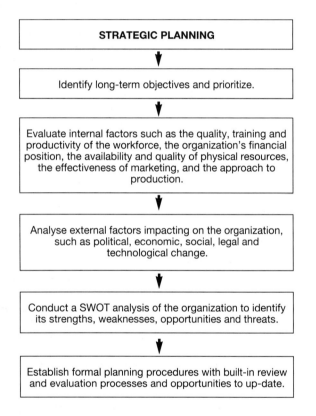

1   It may start at the top of an organization, with a planning committee setting strategic objectives and formulating plans. These would then be handed down to departments to determine their own strategic objectives.
2   It may start at the bottom of an organization, with departments producing their own plans. These would then form the basis of the plan put forward by the planning committee.

The first method has the advantage of fully utilizing planning skills, but the disadvantage of sometimes being considered to be imposed. The second has the advantage of involving everyone in the planning process, thus providing a wider planning perspective and drawing upon the planning skills of a more extensive group of the workforce. However, in reality there is the danger that some planning committees may only pay lip-service to the wishes of departments.

The position of strategic planning within the overall planning process is clearly shown in the first of the following diagrams.

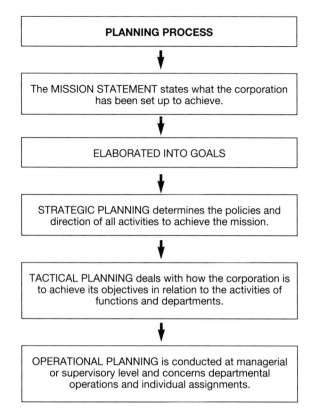

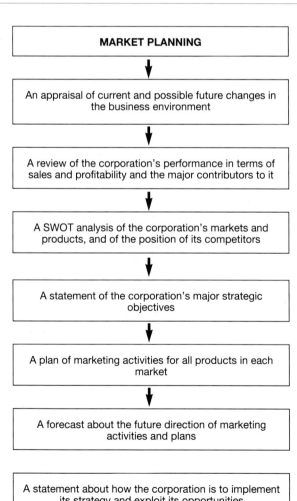

The marketing plan

An integral part of strategic planning is the marketing plan. It represents the natural starting point for the whole planning process. Until it has been constructed it is difficult to produce useful plans for the other company functions such as production and finance.

Because of the changing nature of the business environment there is generally little point in producing a marketing plan in anything more than an outline for three to five years ahead and in detail for six months ahead.

The plan usually covers the stages shown in the figure above. There needs to be a detailed planning cycle that indicates a deadline and time allowance for each stage.

Microsoft's approach to business planning for change
Operating in a changing environment

During the nineteen years of its existence Microsoft has had to contend with major changes within the business environments of the United States and the rest of the world. It has experienced two major domestic and world recessions with resultant high levels of unemployment. It has witnessed the growth and development of the global company, with business values and methods of operation quite different from those of national companies. Over those nineteen years, the European Community has been expanding and growing in strength, and more recently moving towards the establishment of a single market. The communist bloc has broken up and markets are opening up in Eastern Europe. Dramatic changes have occurred in the application of technology to transport, communications, the media, banking, medicine, production, distribution, the office and education. The make-up of the household has changed as a result of the shift in the roles of men and women and changes in the institution of marriage.

The Microsoft Corporation has successfully ridden with the changes and in certain cases, as with technology, actually contributed to them. From its inception, Microsoft has been associated with technological firsts. It was originally set up to exploit commercially the development work carried out by Bill Gates and Paul Allen in adapting Basic for use on a personal computer. Then in 1983 it announced Windows, an extension to the MS-DOS operating system, which provided a universal operating environment for developing bit-mapped application programmes. Windows represented one of the most significant technological developments of the 1980s. At the start of the following decade, the Microsoft® Ballpoint® Mouse was put on board the space shuttle Discovery. It was selected by the National Aeronautics and Space Administration (NASA) because its design was such that it did not require modification in zero gravity.

During its nineteen years' history, Microsoft has also recognized and planned for market opportunities stemming from political change, and in January 1993 it was able to open a wholly owned subsidiary, Microsoft AO, in Moscow.

Microsoft has also successfully responded to Government-backed initiatives. For example, in July 1993 with the American Environmental Protection Agency's announcement of a logo to promote energy-efficient computer systems, Microsoft emphasized its commitment to provide customers with software that supports energy efficiency.

Microsoft's ability to respond to the changing environment has been due to its grasp and commitment to sound planning. The starting point for that planning has been its mission. Microsoft was founded with a vision of 'a computer at every desk and in every home'.

In other words, it has had a commitment to break down the technological barriers and the mystique surrounding the computer and to make it accessible to everyone in both the home and the working environment.

Business start-up

Microsoft grew out of a research and development project. It was only after Bill Gates and Paul Allen had adapted Basic that they really tried to exploit its market potential.

They already had a customer – MITS of Albuquerque, New Mexico, manufacturer of the Altair personal computer – before they formally set themselves up as a partnership. Obviously, this made it relatively easy to get started and to plan for the future. They then refined their product in line with the mission statement to make it accessible to a wider range of customers, including General Electric, NCR and Citibank. With a proven product, finance for the business was easier to acquire and growth through planned product development took place more rapidly.

The operation expanded and market recognition was achieved, and in 1981 the business became incorporated. In 1986 it enjoyed the additional financial benefits of going public.

Strategic planning

The mission and goals

The rapid growth and development of Microsoft have been due to its clear mission statement and the long-term vision that has allowed it to fulfil that mission. Its entire planning process is clearly focused on the future, and responds to the changes that are continually occurring in the business environmental and the market.

In support of its mission Microsoft has identified three main goals for the 1990s:

1   to produce powerful and useful products that help people do their jobs more quickly and effectively;
2   to make it easier for people to get the most out of their software by providing a wide range of support services that recognize individual and corporate needs;
3   to help Microsoft employees to reach their full potential within the corporation and in the communities where they live (the latter involves providing financial support for community projects undertaken by Microsoft employees).

These goals have been translated into Microsoft's overall strategic plan.

Long-term objectives for the 1990s

Underpinning the strategic plan is the long-term objective of the chairman, Bill Gates, to deliver 'information at your fingertips'. This is the idea of making personal computers even more personal – in fact making them indispensable, something that people would reach for automatically if they were in need of any sort of information. This involves thinking about technology from the point of view of the individual user. It means considering how people work and think, and what they need in order to work and think more effectively.

This market-orientated approach clearly demonstrates that Microsoft has identified the needs of the market and has put its marketing plan at the very heart of its strategic plan.

Evaluation of internal factors

As part of its strategic planning for the 1990s, Microsoft appraised every aspect of its internal operations. It recognized that since its products have a global market it needs a global operation.

It is clear that the workforce meets this requirement because in 1992 Microsoft employed 12,000 people in twenty-seven countries around the world.

Increasingly, production is being shifted from traditional manufacturing lines to quality-focused round tables where each individual has greater responsibility for the finished product. This effectively empowers groups of workers all around the world and in so doing raises productivity and efficiency.

Microsoft's physical resources are clearly suitable for a global operation. For example, its corporate network has more than 20,000 personal computers linked through 3,330 miles (5,360 km) of cabling as well as international extensions.

Microsoft takes a global approach towards the market. It is innovative, flexible and willing to change. For example, in 1992 it produced forty-eight new products. It also prides itself on its sales support operation, which employs some 2,000 people who answered 4.6 million calls in 1992. Microsoft has also established its own consulting service which helps customers worldwide to make the most of Microsoft Windows.

Analysis of external factors

The chairman's vision of 'information at your fingertips' clearly demonstrates how he recognizes the changing face of the external business environment. He recognizes how economic, political and social pressures are demanding improvements in efficiency and productivity in the areas of work, education and leisure. He feels that the manner in which business will need to be conducted, the home organized and educational information provided means that computer applications will have to be integrated, the hardware will have to become really portable and one overall computer language established.

SWOT analysis

Microsoft is constantly analysing its strengths, weaknesses, opportunities and threats. These may be classified as follows:

1 Strengths
   • product innovation
   • customer satisfaction
   • quality of workforce

2 Weaknesses
   • the pace at which complementary technologies keep up with Microsoft's drive for development

3 Opportunities
   • those that are clearly recognized in the vision of 'information at your fingertips'.

4 Threats
   • the possible failure of complementary technologies to keep pace with Microsoft

Formal planning procedures

Microsoft is constantly reviewing and updating its plans in an effort to maintain its position in the market-place. For example, in order to achieve its strategic objectives it altered its methods of operation in 1992 and reshaped the Corporation, structuring it under three main groups:

• Products
• Sales and support
• Operations

These three groups report through the Office of the President. It is felt that this new structure will allow Microsoft to work more efficiently and provide the best possible support to customers, while encouraging the workforce to think globally.

Activities

Short-answer questions

1 To what extent has Microsoft developed from being a product-orientated operation to one more concerned with the market-place?
2 Explain how well-planned diversification has been the key to Microsoft's success.
3 Identify three major factors that have contributed towards Microsoft's rapid growth and success during the past nineteen years.
4 Discuss the view that Microsoft has led technological development and in so doing has managed to keep ahead of the competition.
5 Describe how Microsoft has developed into a global corporation.
6 Give two advantages that Microsoft had when it set up in business?
7 Explain how strategic planning at Microsoft starts at the very top.
8 Analyse Microsoft's mission and its relevance for the 1990s.

Media assignment

Read the article at the top of the following page, which has been taken from Microsoft Magazine, Volume 3, Issue 4, Spring/Summer 1993, and then complete the tasks.

Tasks

1 Identify the unique selling points of Windows for Workgroups 3.1.
2 How does the product reflect Microsoft's vision of 'information at your fingertips'?

Windows for Workgroups strikes chord in peer-to-peer market

Microsoft® Windows™ for Workgroups 3.1, which began shipping only last autumn, has secured more than 30 per cent of total UK Windows retail sales. The figure does not include pre-installations by original equipment manufacturers on their machines.

'Current figures indicate that Windows for Workgroups has an 80 per cent share of sales made by resellers here,' said Andy Brown, market monitoring manager at Romtec. 'Windows for Workgroups has already captured a significant 15 per cent share of the network operating system market through resellers, but where it has had the greatest impact is in opening up the peer-to-peer market.'

Sales of Windows for Workgroups have even exceeded Microsoft's expectations. 'This enormous demand proves users need a product that combines the ease of use of Windows with networking, which is traditionally seen as complex,' said David Bridger, product manager for workgroup systems at Microsoft. 'The sales of 20 and 100 user licence packs indicate that Windows for Workgroups is going into a lot of larger groups within enterprises, in addition to small businesses.'

'Windows for Workgroups has significantly changed the way we work. Our office has six PCs running word processing, spreadsheets and some custom applications, but we never had the capability to share information, and applications such as mail seemed very futuristic. Since installing Windows for Workgroups, we have eliminated tons of paperwork and hundreds of man-hours.'
Tom Purcell, Sharp & Purcell, Solicitors

'We have found two overall benefits from using Windows for Workgroups. Schedule+ is a big bonus. And we can now monitor software and configure files of individual PCs through the central server. This used to be done manually, but now we don't have to disrupt our users, so we can save two or three man-days a month.'
Roger Kelly, senior systems development manager, Barclays Bank

Microsoft's Role

If there is any pattern to what we are seeing today, it is that information is becoming more and more complex, and integrating it is becoming more and more important. All these new technologies await us. Unless they are implemented in standard ways on standard platforms, any technical benefits will be wasted by the further splintering of the information base. True, notebook computers, for instance, are just beginning to emerge, as hardware manufacturers rapidly advance flat-screen technology. If these machines are incompatible with existing standards, they will simply create a small niche in the market because the huge mass of existing PC applications will not be able to take advantage of them. Microsoft's role is to move the current generation of PC software users, which is quickly approaching 60 million, to an exciting new era of improved desktop applications and truly portable PCs in a way that keeps users' current applications, and their huge investment in them, intact.

Our goal is to evolve the existing PC system standards to include new capabilities such as compound documents, object-oriented file systems, distributed file systems, handwriting recognition, and multimedia. A nonstandard implementation might offer a short-term time advantage for a particular feature, but a better solution would be to incorporate new technologies directly into the PC architecture or systems software. If the goal is to unify all the information in our lives, then we must bring the standard along carefully so that all the users come along.

Because all the requirements· for **Information at your fingertips** are interrelated, Microsoft's role is key: we are positioned to solve many of these problems at a fundamental level, in the underlying operating system. The ability to have a file system that stores objects, to have different objects know how to act on one another, to locate things wherever in the world they may be, to tie together applications and to share various functions such as charting and outlining across applications, to expand these efforts into new kinds of technology such as notebook computers and multimedia machines in the home – Microsoft is in a unique position to unify all those efforts. As developers of operating systems and networks, we are required to take a broader view, not just so our applications can run, but so an entire industry can prosper and a whole generation of users can make the technological leap into the future.

This broad vision will take several years to unfold. We will introduce capabilities over time in order to bring the user community along without disruption. Each step will need to preserve compatibility. At each step we will work with independent software developers as we did when we developed Microsoft Windows and as we and IBM did when we developed OS/2. Tremendous synergy will develop when large numbers of applications and information objects have been implemented according to the standards we are developing. We are excited to be developing software that will let users automate the handling of daily tasks and information processes without writing a single line of code, but simply by showing the system what they want done. We are excited to be developing software that will let users search for information from a greater range of sources than is possible today and that will let them file and retrieve things more quickly and efficiently than they can today. We are excited to be developing software that will let users create information with greater richness and diversity than anything that can now be done on paper or with current computer technology. We are excited that we can enable users to solve problems that up until now could not be solved.

But Microsoft cannot do this alone. Fulfilling this promise requires the cooperation of the PC industry and information providers. Together we can deliver the computing systems that can do all this.

Case study

The statement at the bottom of the previous page is part of a general text outlining Microsoft's vision of 'Information at your fingertips'. Study it carefully and then complete the tasks.

Tasks

1　Explain how this vision of Microsoft's future role fits in with its overall strategic plan.
2　Identify the potential threats that exist to the achievement of these objectives.

Local investigation

1　Divide the class into three groups with responsibility for investigating the role of the computer in the working, home or educational environment.
2　Each group should design a suitable questionnaire and conduct a survey of its areas of investigation in order to discover how people feel computers should be applied in the future.
3　The class should combine its findings and compare them with Microsoft's vision of 'information at your fingertips'.

Index

Compiled by INDEXING SPECIALISTS, 202 Church Road, Hove, East Sussex BN3 2DJ.